WITHDRAWN

SEMINAR STUDIES IN HISTORY

Editor: Patrick Richardson

The Scramble for Africa

SEMINAR STUDIES IN HISTORY

Editor: Patrick Richardson

A full list of titles in this
series will be found on the
back cover of this book

SEMINAR STUDIES IN HISTORY

The Scramble for Africa

M. E. Chamberlain

LONGMAN

LONGMAN GROUP UK LIMITED
Longman House,
Burnt Mill, Harlow, Essex CM20 2JE, England
and Associated Companies throughout the world.

© Longman Group Limited 1974

First published 1974
Tenth impression 1988

Produced by Longman Group (FE) Ltd
Printed in Hong Kong

ISBN 0-582-35204-5

Contents

Introduction to the Series

The seminar method of teaching is being used increasingly. It is a way of learning in smaller groups through discussion, designed both to get away from and to supplement the basic lecture techniques. To be successful, the members of a seminar must be informed — or else, in the unkind phrase of a cynic — it can be a 'pooling of ignorance'. The chapter in the textbook of English or European history by its nature cannot provide material in this depth, but at the same time the full academic work may be too long and perhaps too advanced.

For this reason we have invited practising teachers to contribute short studies on specialised aspects of British and European history with these special needs in mind. For this series the authors have been asked to provide, in addition to their basic analysis, a full selection of documentary material of all kinds and an up-to-date and comprehensive bibliography. Both these sections are referred to in the text, but it is hoped that they will prove to be valuable teaching and learning aids in themselves.

Note on the System of References:

A bold number in round brackets (**5**) in the text refers the reader to the corresponding entry in the Bibliography section at the end of the book.

A bold number in square brackets, preceded by 'doc' [**docs 6, 8**] refers the reader to the corresponding items in the section of Documents, which follows the main text.

PATRICK RICHARDSON
General Editor

Acknowledgements

I should like to acknowledge my debt to Dr. A.F. Madden of Nuffield College, Oxford, who first aroused my interest in Commonwealth studies, Professor G. Shepperson of the University of Edinburgh who has always kept a friendly eye on the development of Commonwealth and African courses in University College, Swansea, Professors Glanmor Williams and Alun Davies of University College, Swansea, and particularly my colleague, Mr. Neville Masterman, who has listened so patiently to me and to my research students, and finally to Mr. Patrick Richardson, the general editor of the series, for his painstaking scrutiny of the manuscript.

I should also like to thank Mrs. Glenys Bridges of the Geography Department, University College, Swansea for the maps, Mrs. P.M. Thomas and the secretarial staff of the History Department, especially Mrs. Kathleen Rees, for the typing and my father for his help in preparing the manuscript and compiling the index.

M.E. Chamberlain

We are grateful to the following for permission to reproduce copyright material:

George Allen & Unwin Ltd. for an extract from *Imperialism* by J.A. Hobson, Cambridge University Press for an extract from *New Cambridge Modern History*, Vol. XI by R. E. Robinson and J. Gallagher (1962) and H.M.S.O. for extracts from Crown Copyright material. The cover print is reproduced by permission of the *Mansell Collection.*

PART ONE

The Background

1 The African Background

European understanding of African history has undergone a revolution in the last twenty years. A generation ago reputable scholars could write: 'For countless centuries, while all the pageant of history swept by Africa remained unmoved in primitive savagery' (3), or 'Perhaps in the future there will be some African history to teach. But at present there is none: there is only the history of Europeans in Africa. The rest is darkness. . . . And darkness is not a subject of history' (88). In this they were echoing their Victorian predecessors. The explorer, Sir Samuel Baker, told a Victorian audience in 1874

Central Africa . . . is without a history. In that savage country . . . we find no vestiges of the past – no ancient architecture, neither sculpture, nor even one chiselled stone to prove that the Negro savage of this day is inferior to a remote ancestor. . . . We must therefore conclude that the races of man which now inhabit [this region] are unchanged from the prehistoric tribes who were the original inhabitants.

The distinguished colonial administrator, Sir Bartle Frere, with a wide experience of India as well as Africa, did not disagree.

If you read the history of any part of the Negro population of Africa, you will find nothing but a dreary recurrence of tribal wars, and an absence of everything which forms a stable government, and year after year, generation after generation, century after century, these tribes go on obeying no law but that of force, and consequently never emerging from the state of barbarism in which we find them at present, and in which they have lived, so far as we know, for a period long anterior to our own (1).

Only slowly is it becoming apparent how mistaken this view was and that medieval Africa supported civilisations and societies, different from, but as colourful as, those of medieval Europe (5, 6).

This was hidden from Europeans for a variety of reasons. A European is accustomed to study history through written records. For large parts of Africa no such documents exist. Where they do exist, they are generally in Arabic and European scholars have only recently begun to study them seriously. Only in recent years too have archaeological techniques, the use of oral traditions and scientific anthropology become sufficiently developed to make possible the reconstruction of the history of societies which kept no written records. Another difficulty bedevilled European understanding of Africa. Nineteenth century Europe had become so used to seeing political power embodied in national states that Europeans found it almost impossible to recognise any other form of political organisation, and came to regard the absence of identifiable states as proof of anarchy. Even early explorers were, however, impressed by some African art forms. African sculptures, carvings and textiles became known to Europeans at a time when the romantic movement was taking the place of the eighteenth century admiration for classical models and from the beginning their strange and exotic forms attracted some interest (2). But the most important examples of African art became known to Europe comparatively late. The beautiful bronzes and ivories of Benin were discovered in 1897 but they showed clear traces of Portuguese influence. The first of the magnificent bronzes of Ife, the earliest of which date from the thirteenth century and owe nothing to Europe, was not found until 1910 and the main collection did not come to light until 1938 (17). Europeans stumbled on the great stone remains of Zimbabwe in 1868, but it was long supposed that they could not be the work of indigenous Africans and must be the relics of the Phoenicians who, it was surmised, had mined gold in what is now Rhodesia. Radio carbon tests have yielded dates between the fifth and fifteenth centuries AD and combined with other archaeological evidence leave no serious doubt that they were an African creation. The European reaction to the discovery of Zimbabwe was just one striking example of the generally held belief that the African Negro had played a passive part in history, occasionally influenced by Phoenicians, Arabs or other outside peoples, but never himself creative (3, 9).

This picture cannot be sustained in the face of later and more scientific investigations, but men act on the basis of what they believe to be true and it is instructive to compare the Victorian 'image of Africa' with what painstaking, and still incomplete, enquiries have suggested is nearer the truth. Archaeologists, in particular, have centred much attention on Africa in recent years, for Africa may well have the longest human history of any of the continents. If Asia was the cradle of civilisation, as the word is commonly understood today, Africa was very possibly the birthplace of man himself. In the word of one historian, 'Africa was the mother of mankind', the place where *homo*

sapiens first emerged (5). In the Stone Age Africa was 'not even relatively backward: it was in the lead' (10).

The influence of climate on civilisations has fascinated both modern
archaeologists and Victorian scientists. Modern archaeologists would
accept that favourable climatic conditions helped the early emergence
of relatively advanced human groups in Africa. The continent did not
suffer the ravages of the Ice Age as Europe and Asia did. Its history was
influenced rather by alternating 'wet' and 'dry' periods during which
the size of the Sahara desert varied greatly. In the nineteenth century it
was fashionable in some quarters to suppose that climatic conditions
were decisive in determining relative degrees of civilisation. Early
anthropologists thought that all human society developed through three
stages: savagery, characterised by hunting and food-gathering; barbarism, characterised by the emergence of settled agriculture; and
civilisation, characterised by the development of commerce. To some
Victorian observers Africa seemed to have got stuck in the second stage.
They sought explanations for this and found it in the doctrine of
'tropical abundance'. The very richness of Africa had helped the pro-
gression from the first stage to the second but then tended to stultify
progress because a tolerable life could be obtained with comparatively
little effort. Advanced civilisations only appeared in temperate regions
where a high degree of organisation was necessary to ensure adequate
food and shelter. The inhabitants of all tropical regions, not just Africa,
were likely to remain in the stage of 'barbarism'. This was often
coupled with the stock charge that Negroes were naturally 'lazy' and
always did the minimum of work. This seems to have arisen partly
because the picture of the African Negro was drawn from the (often
unfavourable) view that was held of the American slave, partly because
of a failure on the part of early observers to have any appreciation of
the natural rhythms of work of any agrarian community (2).

Despite the gratuitous charge of laziness, it should be remembered
that those who argued this way were essentially environmentalists, not
racialists, that is to say they contended that a particular combination of
geographical and climatic factors had produced a particular, rather
backward, society, not that the genetic endowment of the inhabitants
would have caused them to fall behind the rest of mankind no matter
how favourable their environment had been. Many modern commentators are perhaps not so far removed from this thesis as might appear
at first. Few modern anthropologists or archaeologists would care to
use the crude classification of 'savagery, barbarism and civilisation'.
'Barbarism' is a loaded word (and a relative one: Bernard Berenson
could refer to Italian paintings of the thirteenth century as 'barbaric');

it is plainly better avoided. But Victorian observers were attempting to describe what modern writers would prefer to call a 'high' or 'mature' Iron Age civilisation. For the environmentalist the outlook for the African was necessarily much more favourable than for the racialist. With Victorian confidence in the mastery of man over nature they believed that the environment could be drastically changed.

Environment obviously did play a crucial role in the development of Africa. The Sahara desert was the great divide. The North African littoral looked towards Europe and the Near East. Despite links through the valley of the Nile and trade routes across the Sahara itself, in historic times its development has been very different from that of Africa south of the Sahara. The savanna belt immediately south of the Sahara, or the highlands of East Africa, provided a quite different environment from that of the rain forests of West Africa or of the Congo. In the extreme south of the continent were temperate lands which demanded a quite different form of economy from the tropical regions further north. Deserts and forests formed natural barriers to free communications in some parts of Africa. Africa was also unfortunate in having few easily navigable rivers. The presence of the tsetse fly over large areas of the continent precluded the use of draught animals and meant that goods had to be carried by human porters. All these factors were a severe check to rapid development.

Geographical factors affected the very complex distribution of races in modern Africa. North of the Sahara the earliest known peoples were the ancestors of the modern Berbers but, in historic times, there has been a considerable admixture of Arab blood. South of the Sahara the Bushmen, Hottentots and pygmies are probably derived from the 'aboriginal' stock — so far as that can be guessed at. The origin of the Negro who today dominates most of the continent is not known with certainty but the ancestor of the 'true Negro' may have first appeared in the equatorial forests of West Africa. In northern and eastern Africa there was some immigration of other peoples from western Asia. It has been customary to refer to these peoples as 'Hamitic' but this description has fallen into disfavour with some modern commentators because of Victorian beliefs that these people were 'white' and so, by definition, superior to the Negro — a belief that led to the theory that wherever a more advanced culture appeared in black Africa it must be due to some infusion of 'Hamitic' blood.

Linguistic divisions are sometimes more useful, and meaningful, than racial ones. The most widespread family of Negro languages are the Bantu ones, not always mutually intelligible but clearly deriving from some common original, as Spanish and Italian derive from Latin. The

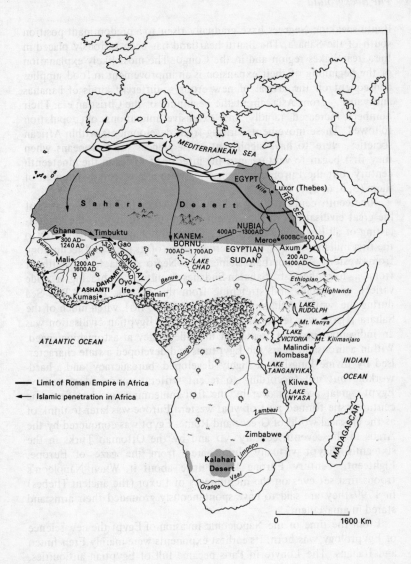

Limit of Roman Empire in Africa

← **Islamic penetration in Africa**

MEDITERRANEAN SEA

S a h a r a   D e s e r t

EGYPT

Luxor (Thebes)

RED SEA

Nile

Ghana
300 AD—
1240 AD

Timbuktu

Gao

NUBIA
400AD—1300AD

KANEM-
BORNU
700AD—1700AD

Meroe
600BC—400 AD

Axum
200 AD—
1400 AD

Senegal

Mali
1200 AD—
1600 AD

Niger

1335 AD—1590 AD
SONGHAY

LAKE
CHAD

EGYPTIAN
SUDAN

DAHOME
Oyo

Benue

Ethiopian

ASHANTI
Ife
Benin

Highlands

Kumasi

LAKE
RUDOLPH

ATLANTIC OCEAN

Mt. Kenya

Congo

LAKE
VICTORIA

Mt. Kilimanjaro

Malindi

Mombasa

INDIAN

LAKE
TANGANYIKA

OCEAN

Kilwa

LAKE
NYASA

Zambesi

MADAGASCAR

Zimbabwe

Kalahari
Desert

Limpopo

Vaal

Orange

0   1600 Km

7

Bantu-speaking Negroes have gradually risen to a predominant position south of the Sahara. The Bantu heartland has been variously placed in the Great Lakes region and in the Congo. The most likely explanation of the beginning of their expansion is an improvement in food supplies consequent on the arrival of new crops — different kinds of bananas and yams — from Asia, about the beginning of the Christian era. Their numbers increased rapidly and extensive migrations of population followed. These movements, arising from developments within African societies, were to have significant consequences for Europeans when they first began to venture into the interior of Africa in the nineteenth century, but the Europeans themselves were almost totally ignorant of them (**3, 5, 6, 8, 9, 10**).

Nineteenth century Europe knew that Africa had produced one of the great civilisations of the ancient world, that of Egypt, the longest-lasting of all high civilisations, its history stretching from the fourth to the first millennium BC. Egypt derived some of its ideas and technology from western Asia, perhaps some from Negro Africa to its south or from a hypothetical 'Saharan-Sudanese' culture embracing a wide variety of peoples and stretching from the Atlantic to the Red Sea during the 'wet' Makalian phase (*c.* 5,500-2,500 BC), when much of the Sahara region was fertile (**5**). But essentially Egyptian civilisation was an indigenous product created in the Nile Valley at astonishing speed. Within a thousand years the Egyptians had developed a state characterised by divine kingship, a highly developed 'bureaucracy' and a hard-working but not (according to recent writers) oppressed peasantry. Egypt's great age was over by the first millennium BC but for some centuries she formed part of what western Europe was later to think of as the classical world of Greece and Rome. Egypt was conquered by the Arabs in the seventh century AD and by the Ottoman Turks in the sixteenth. Egypt virtually disappeared from the gaze of Europe. Eighteenth century Europe knew little about it. When Napoleon's troops first set eyes on the monuments of Luxor (the ancient Thebes) in 1799 they are said to have spontaneously grounded their arms and stared in amazement.

From the time of the Napoleonic invasion of Egypt the new science of Egyptology was born. Its earliest exponents were mainly Frenchmen and Italians. The Louvre in Paris became full of Egyptian antiquities. Later, particularly after the British occupation of Egypt in 1882, Englishmen also became prominent in the field. The whole cult reached its climax with the discovery of Tutankhamen's tomb by Howard Carter and the Earl of Carnarvon in the 1920s. Egyptology reinforced the European sense of the mystery and the richness of Africa. 'From Africa always something new.' Strangely enough it did not increase Europeans' respect for the inhabitants of Africa. They did not really identify the Egyptian fellahin they knew with the authors of the ancient civilisation which fascinated them, even though Victorian anthropologists believed that the Egyptian peasants, both Coptic Christians and Muslims, were the direct descendants of the ancient Egyptians, with comparatively little admixture of Arab blood. The Egyptians themselves were occasionally sufficiently conscious of their past to remind the British during the long British occupation of Egypt that their ancestors had built the pyramids while their conquerors' ancestors were still dressed in woad, but this was the exception not the rule. The European attitude at its extreme was represented by Lord Curzon who could stand in the shadow of the pyramids and ponder seriously on the possibility of 'civilising' the Egyptians (**5, 10, 49, 77**).

The history of Egypt is often not treated as part of the history of Africa and certainly Egypt had vital links with the Mediterranean world and with Asia but it also interacted in important ways with Negro Africa to its south. At the greatest extent of its power Dynastic Egypt had governed what later ages called the Egyptian Sudan, the biblical land of Kush. When Egypt proper succumbed to foreign invaders in the first millennium BC Egyptian civilisation continued in Kush. As Professors Oliver and Fage point out, a development which western historians have seen simply as the slow decline of Egypt was 'according to the very different perspectives of African history . . . ancient Egypt moving nearer to black Africa, at a period when at least part of black Africa was more capable than it had ever been before of experiencing the influence of an urban civilisation'. Kush itself became increasingly a Negro kingdom. It stood at important trade cross roads. It proved to have rich resources of iron ore. An often-quoted early twentieth century archaeologist, Sayce, standing amid the slag heaps of its ancient capital, Meroe, christened it 'the Birmingham of Africa'. Meroe itself declined in the early centuries of the Christian era before the rising power of Axum, which had its centre in the Ethiopian highlands. But it passed on many ideas of Egyptian civilisation, and probably some metal-working techniques as well, to the Negro kingdoms of tropical Africa. These ideas seem to have spread along two main axes, one westwards through the savanna belt lying between the Sahara desert and the equatorial forests, where important states were to rise a few centuries later; another, more problematic, southwards along the highlands of East Africa to the area of the modern Rhodesia (**3, 8, 9, 10**).

A few centuries later, in the seventh century AD, Africa suffered the first of the great alien invasions of historic times, that of the Arabs.

They swiftly overran the whole of Africa north of the Sahara and by the second decade of the eighth century had reached the Atlantic coast of Morocco and had begun the invasion of Spain. Farther south they were checked by the Christian kingdom of Nubia, the heir of Kush, which did not finally collapse until the fourteenth century. Another Christian kingdom, Abyssinia, the successor to Axum, never surrendered, and remained an isolated island of Christianity in the surrounding sea of Islam (8, 9). Faint memories of Abyssinia, the fabled land of Prester John, remained in Europe. Apart from that, Europeans had little idea of what was happening in Africa. A few centuries later another wave of Arab invaders passed south of the Sahara along the Sudanic belt. Physically the Arab presence was always a limited one in this region but the ideas of Islam made rapid headway. The adoption of Islam involved far less of a 'culture shock' for many Negro peoples than Christianity was to be later. In particular it required no fundamental upheaval of family structure, since polygamy was permitted. The adoption of Islam had certain distinct advantages. It brought people into the great diplomatic and trading world which stretched from the Atlantic to China (16).

The savanna belt supported a number of states, or 'empires', in the period which corresponded to the Middle Ages in Europe. They attained a high degree of organisation and urban civilisation. Among these empires one of the earliest and most interesting was that of Ghana. Geographically, it lay well to the north of the present state of Ghana, but a tradition, accepted by some modern scholars and rejected by others, traced a major migration of peoples from ancient to modern Ghana. Unquestionably the adoption of the ancient name by the citizens of what, in colonial times, had been known as the Gold Coast, represented a desire to identify themselves with what they felt to be their own indigenous past, before it had been rudely interrupted by foreign invasions. Historic Ghana was, according to tradition, founded about AD 300. It was a great iron-working centre. It also stood at a most important trade crossroads. Gold came from the mines to the south and was exchanged for the salt of the Sahara. Ghana was essentially a Negro creation, though there may have been some diffusion of culture from the Berbers across the Sahara. When the Arabs arrived in force in the eleventh century, their writers testified to its military strength and the splendour of its capital.

Another great savanna empire was that of Mali (its name too has been adopted by a modern African state) which flourished between the thirteenth and the seventeenth centuries, probably reaching its height in the fourteenth. Mali burst on the attention of an astonished world in the 1320s when its ruler, Kankan Musa, went on a pilgrimage to Mecca. Arab writers recorded the splendour of his entourage. He took so much gold to Cairo that the Egyptian currency was undermined and had to be revalued. Not surprisingly he became known as the 'King of the Gold Mines'. This was not strictly true. Mali, like Ghana, was essentially a trading state, but its economy was highly developed and its chief city, Timbuktu, was already a legend. Modern writers have compared it to the cities of medieval Italy as a centre of learning and commerce.

Slightly younger than Mali was Songhay, another trading state with its capital at Gao, which included the Hausa states of what later became Northern Nigeria, and which seems to have succeeded to Mali's position when the latter declined. Apart from these three, the history of which is becoming increasingly clear, there was the more obscure empire of 'Kanem-Bornu', which seems really to be a blanket term to cover a series of states which flourished from the eighth to the sixteenth century in an area through which migrants and ideas passed steadily. Archaeological evidence suggests that it attained a high degree of technical skill and there may have been important cultural interaction with Christian Nubia (3, 5, 8, 9, 10, 33).

The savanna belt was a great highway of trade from the Nile to the Niger and beyond. It also lay athwart the trade routes from the North African littoral, across the Sahara to the great mineral riches of the Guinea coast. Lake Chad was at the centre of many of these routes, earning from one writer the all too memorable soubriquet of the 'Clapham Junction' of West Africa. These routes were determined by permanent geographical facts and when, in the late nineteenth century, the European powers tried to open the region to their own commerce they found themselves contending for the same strategic advantages as many generations of their African predecessors, although playing in the process a curious game of 'blind man's buff', since they rarely had adequate information.

One problem exercised European commentators when, in modern times, they first gained some understanding of these savanna empires. Were they 'African' or 'Arab' civilisations? A later generation of writers has come to see this question as essentially meaningless. Some of these states, notably Ghana, antedated the coming of Islam. Others do seem to have reached their greatest prosperity after their ruling classes were converted to Islam, but only a limited number of Arabs penetrated the region. They intermarried freely with, and were absorbed by, the indigenous Negro population. Undoubtedly they derived many ideas from the common stock of Islam, just as the nations of northern Europe derived many of their ideas from the common stock of Christianity which came originally from the Mediterranean, but they adapted and modified them to their own requirements and created their own culture in so doing. This fruitful contact continued until the seventeenth century, when a series of events seems to have cut off these savanna empires from the heartland of Islam in the Near East. This fortuitous severing of links may have had disastrous consequences for West African development. As Basil Davidson puts it, 'never isolated from the medieval world – the world of Arab greatness – the Sudan became isolated from the post-medieval world, the world of technical advance and industrial revolution' (3).

How much did medieval or renaissance Europe know of these contemporary African empires? Clearly, a certain amount. The Arab conquest of the North African coast had severed older European trade links with west Africa across the Sahara which had existed in classical times. But a few Arabs, for one reason or another, passed information on to Europeans, and Jews had a degree of freedom of travel in both societies. Some important Arabic accounts, notably those of the geographer al-Bakri and the traveller Ibn Battuti, were available in the West but were virtually unused because of the language difficulty. Al-Idrisi, who had lived for some time at the court of Roger of Sicily in the eleventh century also wrote in Arabic but his writings became available in Latin in the seventeenth century. But the best known account was the *Description of Africa*, written by Leo Africanus, an Arab from the Maghrib who had travelled extensively in Africa before he became a Christian prisoner of war. This was published in Italian in the middle of the sixteenth century and translated into English in 1600. Something of the history of North Africa was known from the work of Luis del Marmol Carvajel, who wrote in Spanish using Arab sources in the late sixteenth century. The Catalan map of 1375, emanating from a Jewish school of cartographers on Majorca, showed Timbuktu, Mali and Gao in roughly the correct places. It is possible that Henry the Navigator was inspired to send Portuguese sailors to explore the coast of Africa in the fifteenth century, not only to find a route to the spice islands of the East but also to make contact with these African kingdoms. Nothing new of much significance was published after the sixteenth century, but memories still coloured European observation of West Africa as late as the eighteenth century. They were not greatly impressed by the African peoples they met on the coast, but legend still spoke of great kingdoms in the interior and writers were forced to posit 'degenerate' peoples on the coast and purer survivals inland (2, 3).

Another part of Africa which was deeply affected by Islam was the east coast. Just as North Africa traditionally looked across the Mediterranean to Europe, so East Africa looked across the Red Sea and the Indian Ocean to Arabia, India and even China. There is ample archaeological evidence that a great Indian Ocean trading complex involving East Africa long antedated Arab conquests. But the incorporation of the East African coast into the Islamic system in the thirteenth century gave a new impetus to trade. Great cities, Kilwa, Mombasa and Malindi, were built on the coast. Here, as in the Sudan, it is sterile to ask whether this was an Arab or an African civilisation. The predominant racial type was Negro, but Negroes who had adopted Arab dress and names along with the Islamic religion. Davidson suggests that the relationship between East Africa and Arabia was not unlike that between England and Renaissance Italy. Ideas and culture flowed from the one but were adapted by the native genius of the other. The trading cities of the coast were the intermediaries between the African hinterland (although apparently without exercising any political control there) and the ocean trading routes. Africa imported textiles and other goods from India. She exported gold and ivory. Slavery always formed a minor item in this trade, but in the late eighteenth century there was a great expansion in the Arab slave trade and, for the first time, raiding parties penetrated deep into the interior of Africa to obtain slaves in large numbers, disrupting the life of many communities in the period immediately before the arrival of Europeans in the interior (3, 10).

If the Arab slave trade disrupted East Africa, on the west coast there had been the long drawn out agony of the Atlantic slave trade. Almost all the maritime nations of western Europe participated. Estimates of the numbers thus transported vary greatly. Between fifteen and twenty million seems a possible estimate. Slavery of a limited and domestic kind was already an established institution in African society when the Europeans arrived, but this represented a drain of healthy young men and women of a totally different order. Apart from those actually transported an unknown number died as the result of the intertribal conflicts which the trade provoked (4, 9, 14, 33).

But it is as well to remember that if the Europeans were the buyers, Africans were the sellers. Europeans did not venture inland to capture their slaves as the Arabs did, but bought what the Africans brought to the coast to await shipment. It used to be believed that Europeans were so·slow to penetrate into Africa because of climatic and geographical difficulties. It is now generally accepted that these were no greater than those which Europeans encountered and overcame in Central America. It was the strength of African political organisation, at least in West Africa, which kept the Europeans on the coast so long. The Africans supplied the goods the Europeans wanted, whether it was slaves or gold.

The Europeans knew that the gold mines lay a bare hundred miles from the coast, but they never saw them (2, 44). Between the Europeans and the African merchants conditions of equal trading partners prevailed. Some commentators have suggested that the slave trade, morally repugnant though it was, did act as an important stimulus as well as an instrument of destruction on the West Coast. The slave trade period saw the rise of Benin, Oyo, Dahomey and the Ashantee Confederation. The appearance of European ships along the Guinea coast certainly altered the direction of trade. Previously the mineral wealth of the coast had gone north to the trading cities of the savanna belt and even across the Sahara to North Africa; now it went south to the sea (9, 10, 33).

The southern tip of Africa presented an entirely different picture from East or West Africa. Here there were no obstacles to European penetration. The climate was temperate and the hinterland accessible; above all, the region was uninhabited apart from some wandering groups of Bushmen and Hottentots. Bartholomew Diaz landed near the cape of Good Hope in 1488, but the Portuguese never made much use of the Cape region as a staging post to the East. They preferred to call at East African ports like Mozambique. It was their successors, the Dutch, who established a base at Table Bay in 1652. This was intended only as a service station for ships of the Dutch East India Company going to and from the East, but a few company employees remained at the Cape after their discharge and began to farm. A number of settlers, many of them French Huguenots fleeing from the Revocation of the Edict of Nantes, came out. By the middle of the eighteenth century settlement stretched three hundred miles east of Cape Town. They met with no serious resistance from the Hottentots. The Company neither encouraged nor resisted their actions and the land was in practice free. In the 1770s the eastward advance reached the Great Fish River. For the first time the Boer settlers encountered stiff resistance. Quite unknowingly, they had bumped into another stream of settlers coming south. These were the vanguard of the Bantu-speaking Africans. In the words of one historian, 'The free land had run out, and Africa was no longer endless. . . . The contact now was between two well-organised societies both of which were based on cattle and both of which required ever-broadening lands in order to survive' (81), or as another puts it, even more pungently, 'When the gap filled by this race was at last closed, strong-armed cattle-rustlers on each side of the border at last met their match' (59).

The Bantu advance had already gone on for over a thousand years. Some historians have suggested that the 'Dark Ages' of the East African coast, between the fourth and the tenth century, when little is known of its history, mark the period when the Bantu settled along the coast line of the modern Kenya and Tanzania. The scanty sources available seem to suggest a change in the racial composition of the people of the coast **(10)**. The Bantu had passed the Zambesi by the fourteenth century and had settled in the Transvaal by the sixteenth. By the early eighteenth century different groups had passed east and west of the Drakensberg Range and had settled in Natal and in the area east of the Great Fish River.

They were a highly organised, essentially warlike, people. They treated the Hottentots whom they found in their path as cavalierly as the Boers did. Even now it is extremely difficult to follow either their movements or their politics in detail, but from time to time they threw up leaders of exceptional talent. The first of these to make an impression on European observers was Shaka, a splendid military tactician who earned the nickname 'the Black Napoleon'. Under Shaka the Zulus, who were in origin only one clan of the Nguni, the Bantu who had occupied the Transvaal region in the sixteenth century, became one of the most formidable fighting forces in southern Africa. A quarrel between Shaka and one of his lieutenants, Mzilikazi, led to the latter leading his followers, who became known as the Matabele, northwards out of Shaka's domains into the land of the Mashona, the modern Rhodesia. Possibly Mzilikazi turned northwards only because it was the most convenient direction to take to escape the wrathful Shaka. Northward movements were not unprecedented in the long saga of Bantu wanderings. But it may also have reflected a realisation that the southern frontier was closing. Donald Morris sums up the Bantu situation dramatically.

> History had offered them a continent ... and they had dallied a little too long. When Van Riebeeck landed at the Cape in 1652, the nearest Bantu were 500 miles to the north and 1,000 miles to the [east] and in this generous toehold the newcomers flourished, so that when the two civilisations finally met ... the Bantu encountered not an artificial colonial outpost but a fully-fledged vigorous folk, rooted and growing, with a vested interest in its hinterlands. Because they did not know they were in a race with a continent for a prize, the Bantu lost it. The hare, in the twinkling of a century, had outstripped the tortoise **(81)**.

The result was an endless and dreary succession of 'Kaffir' wars on the border where the two peoples met. These in turn had a profound effect on Boer psychology for they continued to see the Bantu as something alien to their society, the enemy beyond the frontier even when economic pressures had compelled them to draw their rivals into their own society as a labour force — in the striking metaphor of De Kiewiet, 'the pressures of white colonization pumped them [the Bantu] into every artery and limb of South Africa's social body, until they could not be drained from it safely' **(60)**.

2   The Victorian Image of Africa

The misunderstandings that bedevilled race relations in southern Africa were no doubt aggravated by the peculiarly introspective and self-sufficient nature of Boer society, but they found echoes all over the continent. Europeans in the nineteenth century were almost totally ignorant of all but a few small corners of Africa. Until late in the century they knew practically nothing of the geography or the peoples of its interior. When they spoke – as they frequently did – of the 'Dark Continent', they properly meant a continent which was dark to them, about which they knew little. But this idea merged imperceptibly with another more sinister idea of 'Darkest Africa', Negro Africa, a place of savagery and brutality. Circumstances seemed to conspire to increase misunderstandings.

When Europeans first penetrated into Africa south of the Sahara a number of African communities were in decline. The Atlantic slave trade in the west and the Arab slave trade in the east accounted for some of this, but other African states, like the savanna empires, seem to have declined for purely local reasons. It is possible that the 'Balkanisation' of Africa was more extreme in the middle of the nineteenth century than it had been for centuries. If it is true that it was African strength which had kept the European on the coast in the past, this may itself be a contributory factor in the timing of the European 'opening up' of Africa. Probably, though, this was secondary to another factor, the enormous technological gap which had appeared between European and African civilisations. When the Portuguese first reached the Congo in the late fifteenth century they found a powerful and well-organised state. In the sixteenth century cordial relations developed between the two powers. Congolese came to Europe. Portuguese 'experts', including even printers (8), went to the Congo to instruct the inhabitants. Clearly, even then, the Congolese admired European skills but, equally clearly, no unbridgeable gap was felt to exist between the two cultures. This fruitful relationship continued until the Portuguese became more interested in their Brazilian colony and largely lost interest in Africa except as a source of slaves. A few centuries later such a relationship would have been almost unthinkable.

The peasant communities of medieval Europe, even perhaps the towns of Renaissance Europe, were not impossibly far removed from their African counterparts. But Africa had nothing remotely like the urban civilisation of Europe in the period after the industrial revolution. Psychologically the two cultures had moved very far apart, the more so because of the great stress nineteenth century Europeans were prone to put on technological advance. To them it became almost a badge of 'civilisation'.

But Europe had changed at incredible and unprecedented speed in more ways than in technological advance in the centuries after the Renaissance and, perhaps still more, after the scientific revolution of the eighteenth century. Whole ways of thinking had been revolutionised. Rationalism and humanitarianism had made Europe turn its back on much of its own past. Many things which nineteenth century Europeans found shocking in Africa — and which appear equally shocking to the twentieth century — public executions, torture, mutilating punishments such as lopping off the hand of a thief, a prevailing fear of witchcraft, would have been part of the fabric of life to their own recent ancestors. At no moment in time perhaps were Europeans less able to understand African society than at a period of breakneck change in their own in the nineteenth century.

European views of Negro Africa were originally formed during the slave trade era and related particularly to the coast of West Africa. In the eighteenth century West Africa was particularly important to Britain. Britain sent manufactured goods to West Africa to exchange for slaves who were shipped to the West Indies in return for sugar and similar tropical products. Although there are difficulties in accepting, in its simple form, Dr Eric Williams's famous thesis (18) that the profits of this 'triangular' trade provided the capital to support the industrial revolution in Britain (129), it was certainly central to the British economy in a way in which West African trade never was to be again.

West Africa therefore naturally attracted some popular attention. The slave trade itself was necessarily brutalising for all who participated in it. Most Europeans were shocked by their first contact with it (14). Dealing with men as merchandise in this way almost compelled those concerned not to see them as men at all. Paradoxically, however, since they also dealt with the African merchants who sold the slaves, the slavers were among those most able to think of Africans as individuals and not just see them as a stereotype 'Negro' (2).

The agitation for the abolition of the trade in the late eighteenth century cut both ways in forming the image. Some defenders of the trade, and in the next generation those who opposed the abolition of slavery itself in the British empire, argued that the Negro was not fully human, or was such a degenerate form of humanity that slavery was a desirable condition for him. Arguments raged between those who supported the theory of 'polygenesis', that is that the different races of mankind were created separately and were therefore technically different 'species', and the more orthodox believers in 'monogenesis', that the whole human race sprang from a single pair, Adam and Eve, whatever might have happened to its different branches since. It was noticeable, though, that even those who argued for abolition tended to condemn the cruelty of the trade and of the condition of slavery, or to emphasise the spiritual equality of mankind which derived from the common fatherhood of God, and to slide over the difficult question of the temporal equality of the Negro to the white man in this world. Indeed, many abolitionists inclined to take a paternalistic line and to suggest that the Negro must be defended because he could not defend himself, to see him as a child in an adult world (2).

There were a few correctives to the general 'slave' stereotype. There was the literary tradition of the 'noble savage' which had a considerable vogue in the eighteenth century. This was usually applied to the American Indian or the Polynesian, but the Negro occasionally benefited from it. Indeed the first African hero in English literature (leaving aside the difficult question of Othello's colour) was Oroonoko who appeared in 1688. More important than this, real Africans were not totally unknown in England in the eighteenth century. First, there were several thousand personal servants of one kind or another. Some of them had originally been slaves brought from the West Indies, but the famous judgment by Lord Mansfield in Somersett's case in 1772 (15) laid down that no man could be a slave in England whatever his status elsewhere. There were also, perhaps more surprisingly, some fifty African 'trainees' in Liverpool in the 1780s direct from West Africa, learning English and English commercial practices. The scanty information available suggests that the relations of these people with the indigenous population was neither better nor worse than that of any other group of foreigners, generally amicable but prone to occasional friction arising from dislike of strange customs or competition for jobs or girls (2).

If slavery forced men to formulate an attitude towards the Negro, the late eighteenth century also saw an unprecedented flowering of scientific interest. Both geographical and biological enquiries were the fashion. Captain Cook's voyages had solved many long-standing problems concerning the Pacific. A number of men longed to do the same for Africa. The African Association (strictly the 'Association for promoting the Discovery of the Interior Parts of Africa') was founded in 1788, largely under the inspiration of Joseph Banks, the President of the Royal Society, who had accompanied Cook to the Pacific in 1768, with the support of a few personal friends. They were principally interested in the interior of West Africa. Although nothing new had emerged since the accounts, mainly Arabic, of the tenth to the sixteenth centuries (see above, p. 12), these had become widely available in English for the first time in a number of famous collected works in which the eighteenth century excelled. The greatest triumph of the African Association was the despatch of Mungo Park's first expedition, that of 1795-97, which finally established the general direction of the river Niger which had long mystified Europeans (44).

There was also some British government interest in this period when it was looking for possible compensation for the material and prestige losses of the American War of Independence and for strategic positions during the French revolutionary and Napoleonic wars. Mungo Park's second expedition to the Niger, that of 1805, was government-financed. This interest survived into the early nineteenth century. In 1817 a mission was despatched to the king of the Ashantee in his capital at Kumasi, to sign a political and commercial treaty. A member of the expedition, T. E. Bowdich, published a book about it two years later (*Mission from Cape Coast Castle to Ashantee, London, 1819*). This was a meticulous account of Ashantee culture, including beautifully illustrated sections on subjects like architecture and musical instruments. Bowdich did not attempt to disguise the harsh side of Ashantee life, including public executions and the human sacrifices demanded on the death of the king and on certain other occasions, but they were seen in their context as part of a highly organised society.

Generally, however, British interest in West Africa declined during the first thirty or forty years of the nineteenth century, though the Sierra Leone experiment continued. This was the nearest approach to a colony that Britain maintained on the coast at this time, though there were small communities of merchants resident on the Gold Coast and at the mouth of the river Gambia. The Sierra Leone colony was founded in 1787 as a home for freed slaves and was the forerunner of the better-known American experiment in Liberia. Sierra Leone had a chequered early career and played a paradoxical role in the development of British thinking about Negro Africa. It was under frequent attack from the indigenous population of the area, and while it convinced many that, given time, Africans could adopt a European form of civilisation successfully, it also led to increasingly hostile comparisons being drawn between westernised Africans and their still 'primitive' brethren who had been a danger to the colony (2).

Interest in the West Coast revived with the ill-fated 'Niger experiment' of 1841-42. This is always associated with the name of the anti-slave-trade crusader, Thomas Fowell Buxton, although he took many of his ideas from James MacQueen an earlier writer, better known in his own day than in ours (2). Since Britain and the United States had outlawed the slave trade in 1807 and since other European countries had committed themselves, at least nominally, to the same position in 1815, Britain alone of the European powers had made serious attempts to police the West Coast and stamp out the trade. Her success had been limited. As long as slavery continued in the United States and Brazil slavers of various nationalities would try to carry on the contraband trade, and as long as there were customers Africans would sell slaves. A growing body of opinion in Britain believed that only legitimate commerce would stamp out the trade. The African middlemen must have commodities other than human beings to sell to Europe traders. In West Africa a promising beginning had been made with the trade in palm oil, much in demand for soap and for the lubrication of the new machinery now employed in industrial Britain. The Niger experiment was an attempt to expand this. It failed because of the heavy mortality suffered by the expedition (2, 32).

But the principle was of wider application than the Niger. That legitimate trade would drive out the slave trade became a generally held maxim to be applied to the Arab slave trade of the East Coast as well as to the Atlantic trade, which died a natural death with the abolition of slavery in the United States in the 1860s. But it went further. Commerce, it was held, would raise the African standard of life. It was the natural transition from 'barbarism' to civilisation. It was necessary for the advance of Africa and Europeans were increasingly beginning to feel responsible for bringing about such an advance [doc. 2]. It also, of course, promised rewards to European traders and investors, but a historian very sympathetic to Africa, P. D. Curtin, rightly warns against the crude simplification of seeing this philosophy simply as a cover for immediate economic self-interest (2). Among the many theories advanced in the middle of the century there were even some forerunners of Lugard's famous *Dual Mandate*, the hypothesis that the interests of the Europeans and of the Africans were essentially complementary. 'Europe benefited by the wonderful increase in the amenities of life for the mass of her people which followed the opening up of Africa at the end of the nineteenth century. Africa benefited by the influx of manufactured goods, and the substitution of law and order for the methods of barbarism' (120).

Despite its ill-success, the Niger experiment temporarily revived British interest in Negro Africa, especially West Africa, but it was at a much lower intellectual level than the scientific enquiries of Park or Bowdich. The 1840s saw a rash of ephemeral publications, mainly travellers' tales. Curtin remarks that the only excuse for yet another new book seemed to be a story of personal adventure and the accounts became steadily more subjective and more sensational. The nadir was perhaps reached with J. Smith's *Trade and Travel in the Gulph of Guinea* (1851) with chapters such as 'Human Sacrifice — Nailing prisoners, Jack Ketch, Decapitation, cooking and eating human flesh. King Pepple eats King Amacree's heart. . . .' But saturation point was eventually reached. Interest fell off in the 1850s. *Blackwood's* magazine, which had carried much on West Africa in earlier decades, published nothing at all on the subject in the 1850s. The noted traveller Richard Burton wrote in 1845 that people were bored with 'ugly savages' and with 'the monotonous recital of rapine, treachery and murder'. Unfortunately this boredom also extended to much more serious studies. The great compendium of information gathered by the German, Heinrich Barth, first published in English in 1857, sold so badly that the print of 2,250 copies for the first three volumes was reduced to 1,000 for the later volumes (2).

This dismissal of African societies as savage and uninteresting coincided with other developments. The period 1829 to 1859 saw a complete rethinking of biological concepts. This reappraisal went back earlier, in fact, to Linnaeus's work in 1734 and was to culminate in Darwin's *Origin of Species* (1859). Men were fascinated by the 'classification' of natural phenomena; the definition of species and ideas of natural selection and even of evolution were already in the air long before Darwin gave them a coherent form. It was natural that the study of human races should play a part in these enquiries. Old disputes about polygenesis and monogenesis were revived, given special impetus by arguments about the abolition of slavery in the United States. It was understandable that European scholars should conclude that the white or 'Caucasian' races of their own kind were the most highly developed. All men are prejudiced in favour of their own kind and the superior technology of Europe gave the proposition a good deal of plausibility in the nineteenth century. It was easy enough then to rank other races according to their resemblance to Europeans, and physically Negroes were the least like Europeans in their external appearance. (No one, of course, could know in the nineteenth century that blood groups and 'tissue typing' would cut across all racial groups.) This comforting thesis seemed to receive reinforcement from the fact that the Chinese and other Asians, who were more like Europeans, had achieved some degree of civilisation. The Africans at the bottom of the heap seemed to be sunk in savagery.

As ideas of evolution gained a hold on public imagination, men increasingly saw African societies as examples of what their own societies had been in earlier eras, 'contemporary ancestors' in H. A. C. Cairns's phrase (1). This theory at least held out hope that the Africans could improve. Even in the nineteenth century it was attacked from two different sides. First, there were the objections of a man of African descent, the West Indian Edward Blyden, an important figure who has only recently become the subject of serious study. Writing in 1887, he rejected the idea that 'the Negro is the European in embryo ... and that when, by and by, he shall enjoy the advantages of civilisation and culture, he will become like the European; in other words, that the Negro is on the same line of progress, in the same groove, with the European, but infinitely in the rear' (1). A more common type of objection to trying to change Africa was that expressed by a correspondent to *John Bull* in 1823, 'We are expending our thousands and tens of thousands a year: to do what, Sir? To wash the Blackamoor white – monstrous absurdity!' (2).

In fact the British taxpayer had little reason to complain for most of the century that his money was being spent on Africa. The upkeep of the Africa squadron to thwart the remaining slavers cost a certain amount until the 1860s. So did the upkeep of the four British stations on the West African coast, the Gambia, Sierra Leone, the Gold Coast (Cape Coast Castle) and, after 1862, Lagos, but in 1865 a Select Committee of the House of Commons reported that Britain would be well advised to relinquish all her holdings on the West Coast, except perhaps Sierra Leone, which had possibilities as a naval base. Although the recommendations of the Committee were never carried out they faithfully reflect the lack of official interest in Africa in the period immediately preceding the Scramble.

The new interest in Africa in the late nineteenth century was a private, not an official, matter. It is interesting to see both how it differed from, and how it built on, earlier precedents. Many British attitudes to Africa were formed during their long slaving and trading connection with the Guinea coast. What is surprising is how many of these attitudes were set and hardened, rather than modified and corrected, during the decades which saw the great European exploration of the African continent. Many of the basic elements in the eighteenth century connection between Europe and Africa emerge strengthened and reinforced in the late nineteenth century. There is an increasing awareness of the economic possibilities of Africa, a genuine scientific interest, an equally genuine humanitarian interest, but, arising from this mélange, a deep and inexorable misunderstanding growing between Europeans and Africans.

The heirs of the eighteenth century humanitarians were the missionary societies. Missionary endeavour came to most of Africa comparatively late: The great era for the foundation of missionary societies in Britain was the late eighteenth century, but not all of them were at first interested in Africa. Even in Sierra Leone the Church Missionary Society did not begin work until 1806 and the Wesleyan Methodist Mission until 1811. The Wesleyans began work in Ashantiland in 1842. In what later became Nigeria the first permanent mission was established in 1844 by the Church Missionary Society. It is worthy of note that during the early days of the missions on the Guinea coast Africans played a more prominent part than they were to be allowed to do again for several generations. Philip Quaque, a Fante who had been educated in England, was the chaplain at Cape Coast Castle in the late eighteenth and early nineteenth centuries. Rather later Samuel Crowther, a Yoruba who had been rescued from a slave ship and also educated in Britain, became a bishop. In South Africa the Boers had tended to avoid missionary activity among the Africans because of the tattered remnants of the doctrine that a baptised Christian had a claim to civil rights, irrespective of his nationality but the London Missionary Society was active there by 1800. The Church Missionary Society had a small station at Mombasa on the East Coast, staffed by German Lutherans, in the middle of the century. Two of these Germans, Johann Krapf and Johann Rebmann, were the first Europeans to set eyes on Mounts Kenya and Kilimanjaro in 1847. But the classic missionary penetration into the interior of Africa was a phenomenon of the 1880s. The missionary societies, almost without exception, had very effective propaganda machines and the picture they drew of Africa gained very wide acceptance.

Unfortunately, in the opinion of Cairns (1), the missionaries bore a special responsibility for increasing the 'cultural arrogance' of the British public and misrepresenting African society in a way calculated to give rise also to racial arrogance. The reasons are not difficult to discern. The missionaries were entirely dependent on public support and subscriptions to carry on their work. Missionaries were urged to send home detailed reports of their activities and of the conditions they found. These reports were then given a very wide circulation. The breadth of the range they covered may be judged by the fact that the societies found it worth while to run special publications for children and for 'working-class' readers. To gain public sympathy missionaries were inevitably tempted to stress the temporal as well as the spiritual aspects of their work and to represent the life of the unconverted African here on earth as brutal and barbarous. Some resorted to a kind of 'before and after' vignettes, representing the converted African in a much happier condition. This form of propaganda (like the theories of the evolutionists) did at least portray the African as capable of improvement, but it also of necessity denigrated his indigenous culture. African religion was often particularly ill-served by missionary observation. Few tried to penetrate below the surface and ask what rituals and apparent crudities meant to the believer. It was easier to assume that Africans worshipped monkeys and serpents, although one wit did comment that an observer from another planet might, on much the same evidence, come to the conclusion that Christians worshipped lambs and doves in their churches. Against this, however, must be set valuable pioneering work by the missionaries in the study of African languages and, where their prejudices were not too deeply engaged, some of the earliest attempts at scientific anthropology.

If humanitarian impulses produced ambiguous results in nineteenth century Africa, so did science. Many motives drove men into Africa during the great age of exploration, a hope of gain, a love of adventure and just plain curiosity. The last should not be underestimated. The Victorians had intensely enquiring minds. The interior of Africa held the most tantalising mysteries left in the world after the exploration of the Americas, Australia and much of Asia. The public at home shared the thrill of discovery of the man on the spot. Space exploration in the twentieth century has never succeeded in generating a quarter of the enthusiasm that the search for the source of the Nile aroused in the nineteenth. The Victorians loved heroes. R. C. K. Ensor once suggested that Victorian politicians were gladiatorial figures to the public, fulfilling a role that in the twentieth century was taken over by sporting personalities. Explorers and quarrelsome scientists seem to have filled something of the same role. Sometimes national competition entered into it, as in the race between H. M. Stanley and de Brazza to reach Stanley Pool in 1880, or of Lugard and Decoeur to reach Borgu in 1894. But at other times it seems to have been simply a love of a good scrap, as in the eager public anticipation of the expected confrontation between Richard Burton and John Hanning Speke at the British Association meeting in Bath in 1864 to defend their rival views of the source of the Nile, a confrontation prevented by Speke's death by shooting (probably accidental, although the suspicion of suicide has never been completely laid) on the very morning of the meeting.

The exploration of the interior of Africa centred on the four great river systems, the Niger, the Zambesi, the Nile and the Congo. The pioneering work on the Niger had been done long ago by Mungo Park. He was to be followed by Hugh Clapperton, the Lander brothers, William Baikie, René Caillié, the Frenchman who reached Timbuktu in the late 1820s, and the great German explorer Heinrich Barth. The Zambesi was, above all, the territory of David Livingstone who explored much of the course of the river, 1851-56. In another great journey, 1858-64, with John Kirk, subsequently the British consul general at Zanzibar, Livingstone explored the river Shire and discovered Lake Nyasa. His later years were taken up with his almost obsessive search for the headwaters of the Nile. Livingstone was rivalled in his search for the Nile by Richard Burton, who had already made a name for himself for his travels in Arabia and the Horn of Africa, and a young officer, John Hanning Speke, who accompanied Burton on his expedition in 1857-59. Speke returned alone in 1860 and met Samuel Baker and his young Hungarian wife who were travelling up the Nile, also searching for its source. Livingstone's activities also drew in two other men, H. M. Stanley and Lieutenant Lovett Cameron. Stanley was at this time a journalist on the staff of the *New York Herald* and he was sent to look for Livingstone who was believed to be missing near Lake Tanganyika in 1871. He found Livingstone and brought the story out for the world. Livingstone died in 1873, before Cameron, who had been sent out by the Royal Geographical Society, could make contact with him. Cameron carried on with his scientific mission, crossing central Africa from east to west (the first European to do so) and emerging in Portuguese Angola in 1875. Cameron had not attempted to follow the river Congo all the way and, when he heard of Livingstone's death, Stanley determined to do so and settle once for all whether the river 'Lualaba' that Livingstone had sighted was the Congo or the Nile. The result was Stanley's east—west crossing of the African continent between 1874 and 1877. The Germans, Gerhard Rohlfs and Georg Schweinfurth, the Portuguese, Serpa Pinto, and the Frenchman, de Brazza, also contributed much to the exploration of Central Africa in this period (12, 13).

All these men wrote long, and often vivid, accounts of their experiences for their public at home [docs 1, 3, 4, 5]. Read a century later, they exhibit some curious features. Most of them wrote as if they were the first men to penetrate to unknown regions. The African inhabitants were regarded as mere background, 'part of the local fauna'.

At the same time they were very conscious of the possibilities of these 'new' regions. Africa was once again coming to seem an El Dorado. There had always been stories of the wealth of Africa, the legendary kingdom of Prester John or the fabled city of Timbuktu. Africa had been known as a source of gold for centuries — Edward II had struck his coins from African gold. Now the careful reports of men like Lieutenant Cameron [**doc. 3**] seemed to confirm this. Many of these 'prospectuses' that came out of Africa in this period proved false, but the diamonds of Kimberley, which burst on an astonished world in the early 1870s, and the gold of the Witwatersrand, discovered in 1886, were real enough. Men did grow rich in Africa: Cecil Rhodes [**doc. 19**] for example, or Leopold II of the Belgians.

The possibilities seemed unlimited and, behind it all, stood the new Victorian technology, the steam ship, the telegraph and, above all, the railway, which for the first time seemed to promise the real opening up of the interior of Africa, defeating the limitations imposed by the tsetse fly. Men began to 'think big'. It was not coincidental that Africa began to be opened up on a large scale just as the American frontier was 'closing'. Men meant it when they spoke of Africa as the 'new America'. Planning was on a continental scale. The Cape to Cairo railway did not seem an extravagant project to those who had seen the Canadian Pacific or the Union Pacific take shape.

Livingstone himself had been an enthusiast for 'progress' [**doc. 2**]. But Livingstone's enthusiasm had always been tempered, indeed in part forged, by his concern for the African. A few men of the next generation, notably Joseph Thomson (1), shared Livingstone's regard for the African and even, in Thomson's case, questioned whether this kind of progress would be good for the average African. But this was very much the exception. A new sense of racial superiority had emerged in which the European's sense that he had the right to do what he liked with Africa was only one manifestation.

The European explorers of Africa were unquestionably brave men venturing into a situation totally unknown to them. They seldom had men of their own race with them, and they often found their African hosts strange and unpredictable, and feared their hostility. In this situation they created their own image of themselves. They must be wise — sometimes they even resorted to fireworks, musical boxes or electric batteries to overawe surprised tribes and establish their reputation as near-magicians. They must be strong, always keeping their word and never showing physical weakness. They must maintain that British tradition of the 'stiff-upper lip' and never show emotion — this may well be the real explanation of Stanley's strange greeting to Livingstone

27

'Dr Livingstone, I presume' (1). This 'white man's burden' that they created for themselves was not altogether without a good side. Sometimes it involved trivialities, like Harry Johnston's insistence on dressing for dinner in the jungle, but the concept of a 'gentleman', whose word was his bond and who was chivalrous to those weaker than himself, especially towards women, was a very meaningful one to many Victorians and may explain why the British were often far from the worst 'aliens' with whom the Africans found themselves dealing (1).

But there was a much darker side to this growing sense of the gap between the black and the white races. If the white man had a position to maintain, respect for the black man sank lower and lower. There had always been those who preferred the sensational to the objective. Smith's *Trade and Travel in the Gulph of Guinea* has already been quoted. A much greater writer than Smith, Richard Burton also did his share, notably in his *Mission to Gelele, the King of Dahomey* (1864) which had chapter headings very similar to those of Smith. Burton also discussed 'the Negro's place in Nature', which he placed very low, contending that, although a Negro child might be intelligent, he became stupid at puberty, like the great apes. He was also an exponent of the 'Hamitic theory', believing that there had only been progress in Africa where more advanced peoples had penetrated. Burton's theories demonstrably influenced certain politicians, including Lord Derby and even the liberal and enlightened Lord Ripon (1).

But the man who reached by far the widest public was Henry Morton Stanley. It was no accident that Stanley's greeting to Livingstone on the shores of Lake Tanganyika became a Victorian catchphrase, still remembered today, indeed described in a recent issue of the *Radio Times* as one of the four most memorable phrases of the Victorian era. All Stanley's activities took place in a blaze of publicity. He usually had massive Press backing. His expedition to find Livingstone was undertaken for the *New York Herald* (see above p. 26), his transcontinental journey was financed by the *New York Herald* and the *Daily Telegraph* jointly. His best-known books, *How I found Livingstone, Through the Dark Continent*, and *In Darkest Africa* (the very titles give the flavour) ran through numerous editions, including cheap 3s. 6d. ones. *In Darkest Africa* sold 150,000 copies in the English edition alone (like Stanley's other works it was translated into many other languages), and one reviewer commented that 'it has been read more universally and with deeper interest than any other publication of the present year' [doc. 5].

Stanley lectured all over the world, in America and Australia, as well as on the continent of Europe. He was a natural showman. Even his worst public quarrels at the British Association or the Royal Geographical Society only served to focus more public attention on him. Fate could hardly have chosen a worse interpreter of Africa to Europe. Stanley's childhood experiences — he was illegitimate, rejected by his family, brought up in a workhouse of Dickensian horror — were enough to have soured any man. His own character and judgment seem to have undergone a progressive degeneration as a result of years of loneliness, anxiety and malarial fever. There is a great difference between the tone of the first book he wrote describing the British Abyssinian expedition of 1868, in which he posed as a disinterested American observer (he had emigrated from Wales to the United States as a boy) prepared to criticise both the Europeans and the Abyssinians, and his last book describing the Emin Pasha Relief expedition in which he almost exulted at atrocities [doc. 5]. Not everyone admired Stanley. The authorities of Westminster Abbey refused to bury him in the Abbey near Livingstone, as Stanley and his family wished. But, although the discriminating might criticise him, he undoubtedly had the ear of the new literate public which seemed to enjoy sensationalism, especially if it were laced with jingoism. J. A. Hobson, the most cogent of the contemporary critics of the 'new imperialism', exclaimed in disgust, 'Popular education, instead of serving as a defence, is an incitement towards Imperialism; it has opened up a panorama of vulgar pride and crude sensationalism to a great inert mass who see current history and the tangled maze of world movements with dim, bewildered eyes . . .' (117).

Stereotypes are always dangerous, whether of one's own people or of others. Cairns reminds us of Inge's remark, 'If you marry the Spirit of your generation you will be a widow in the next' (1). Nineteenth century Englishmen frequently saw Africa through what Curtin calls 'a haze of cross-cultural misunderstanding' (2) which led to the 'acceptance of views of Africa more prejudicial than factual' (1). Nevertheless, there is an opposite danger, namely that 'the pull of contemporary liberal opinion, opposed to policies of imperialism and racial hegemony, may incline the researcher to select his material in favour of the non-white races' (1). To slide over criticisms of other cultures which one would apply to one's own, can be as patronising as any Victorian attitude (7). Even exaggerated feelings of guilt may be a final fling of Victorian arrogance, for it is to take the white men who ventured into Africa at their own valuation, as masters of their own and Africa's destinies. Often, as the sad tale of the 'Scramble' developed, both individual Europeans and Africans seemed to be at the mercy of forces which they neither understood nor controlled.

PART TWO

Analysis

3   The British Occupation of Egypt, 1882

'It is a nasty business, and we have been much out of luck', the British Foreign Secretary, Lord Granville, wrote to a colleague, Lord Spencer, in June 1882, referring to the tangled situation in Egypt. Few have doubted that the last thing which a British Liberal government, under William Gladstone and pledged to reverse the 'forward' foreign policy of the previous Conservative administration of Benjamin Disraeli, wanted was a military intervention in Egypt in 1882, followed by a prolonged occupation. It has been generally agreed by contemporaries and historians alike that the British cabinet 'muddled' into the Egyptian occupation (35, 96). How then did they get into this situation? A number of very different factors must be taken into account, Egypt's role as part of the Ottoman empire, the newly built Suez Canal and its significance for British communications with India, the investment of European financiers in Egypt and the diplomatic alignments of Europe at this time [docs 6-9].

Although Egypt had been conquered by the Ottoman Turks in 1517, it had always retained some degree of autonomy. Nevertheless, a Turkish ruling class had been introduced into the country and the Turks virtually monopolised the higher administrative and, in particular, army appointments. This was naturally resented by the Egyptians, and the Egyptian nationalist movement of the nineteenth century was anti-Turkish before it was anti-European (66, 100).

The attention of Europe was first directed towards Egypt by the Napoleonic campaign of 1798-99. The reasons for the campaign were complicated, but one motive was certainly to strike at Britain by posing a threat to her comparatively newly acquired Indian empire. From a military point of view the campaign was a disaster but it had far-reaching consequences (49). It caused a change of government in Egypt and it established the French, despite the military *débâcle*, as the dominant European influence in Egypt. The Albanian, Mehemet Ali, who consciously modelled himself on Napoleon, was able to seize power. Mehemet Ali remained a vassal of the Sultan of Turkey but he was an ambitious man who was determined to gain the maximum possible independence for Egypt. He embarked on a campaign of conquest and took much of the (Egyptian) Sudan[1] and Syria. It is possible that he hoped one day to become Sultan (66, 72). In his attempts to 'modernise' Egypt, Mehemet Ali made extensive use of French experts, military, agricultural, educational and others. The Egyptian educational system, which was more advanced than that of many parts of Europe, was modelled on the French system and Egyptian law was codified according to Napoleonic practice. Some Egyptians became interested in French philosophy and political thought. The leader of the 1882 rising, Colonel Arabi Pasha, although no scholar, was surprisingly familiar with the precedents of the 'Great Revolution' of 1789. At first those Egyptians who wanted to change their country were by no means hostile to European influence. On the contrary they saw Europeans as allies against the obscurantist elements in their own society (66, 100, 83).

Unfortunately for the Egyptian reformers their country was so placed strategically that it could hardly avoid becoming a bone of contention to the European powers, especially Britain and France. The Napoleonic campaign had alerted Britain to a possible threat to her Indian empire. Mehemet Ali was known to be a French *protégé*, and in 1840 Palmerston joined with Russia, Prussia and Austria to curb Mehemet Ali's ambitious campaigns against the Sultan, even at the expense of destroying the diplomatic *entente* between Britain and Orleanist France. When the Tsar Nicholas II put forward contingency partition plans to the British ambassador before the Crimean War, he recognised that the area that Britain would wish to acquire would be Egypt. Britain, however, at this time and for many years afterwards, was committed to a policy of preserving the decrepit Ottoman empire intact to avoid the worse international complications which would follow its dissolution (106).

The next great threat to the Ottoman empire came with the Russo-Turkish War of 1877-78. Once again there was talk of a possible partition of the empire. For the first time the debate was known and discussed among the newly educated classes in Egypt, and it has been suggested that it was an important stimulus to the development of national feeling and created the beginning of a demand for what a later generation would call 'self-determination' (100). The Ottoman empire survived the crisis but Britain leased the island of Cyprus from the

---

[1] Sudan unfortunately is an ambiguous term. In English it more usually means, as here, the region of the Upper Nile. In French, 'Soudan' means the whole savanna belt from the Nile almost to the Atlantic. In the absence of any convenient alternative term, this usage is now fairly common in English, too, see above Part One.

Sultan, thus providing herself with a base in the eastern Mediterranean, in ~~return for a guarantee of Asiatic Turkey against Russian expansion.~~ During the 'behind the scenes' negotiations at the Congress of Berlin of 1878 France secured a promise from Britain and Germany that they would not oppose a French occupation of Tunis. France was concerned about the fate of Tunis because it bordered her existing colony of Algeria, the occupation of which had begun as long ago as 1829. France did not take up her option on Tunis until 1881, but the French occupation of Tunis then mortally offended the Sultan (Tunis was still nominally part of his empire) and made cooperation between France and Turkey impossible during the Egyptian crisis of the following year.

The completion of the Suez Canal in 1869 obviously introduced a new element into the situation. Egypt had had a strategic importance for Britain before, especially since the 1840s when the 'overland route' began to be used extensively. This involved going to Alexandria by mailboat, crossing Egypt to Suez and picking up another mail boat for India and the East there. The journey was facilitated when a railway was built (by George Stephenson) from Alexandria to Cairo in the 1850s. This route was too complicated for bulk cargoes but for despatches it was invaluable. It was much used during the Indian Mutiny of 1857. The idea of a canal to connect the Red Sea and the Mediterranean went back to Ptolemaic times but it was only in the middle of the nineteenth century that a Frenchman, Ferdinand de Lesseps, provided the right combination of enthusiasm, technical competence and political influence to get the job done.

From the first the British opposed the building of the canal. For them, any advantage of a more convenient route to India was heavily outweighed by the fact that the Canal might fall into the hands of an enemy. The security of British India depended largely on British command of the seas, but as Lord Palmerston, one of the shrewdest of British Foreign Secretaries, pointed out, control of the high seas was something very different from control of a 200 foot 'ditch' through someone else's territory. The only result of British opposition, however, was that the Canal was finally built by French enterprise and capital, although by Egyptian labour. The British contended, almost up to the actual opening of the Canal, that it was technically impossible to build it. Even when it was open, leading men in Britain, including Gladstone himself, continued to believe that in time of war the Canal would probably be closed and that the vital British route to India was still that round the Cape [docs 6a-e].

The Canal, however, soon came to assume a crucial commercial as well as a military importance. There was an element of coincidence in this. If the age of sail had continued the usefulness of the Canal would have been limited by the uncertainty of the winds in the Red Sea. But about this time important technical developments, the triple marine engine and water condensers, greatly increased the freight-carrying capacity of steamships and, for the first time, made them economic competitors of sailing ships on long voyages. For steamships the Canal was an unalloyed advantage. In 1870 the shipping tonnage passing through the Canal was 436,609: by 1882 it had grown to 5,074,809 tons. Before the First World War it had reached over 20 million tons a year. In 1882 over 80 per cent of this traffic was British [doc. 6a] (34, 73, 93).

Britain plainly could not remain indifferent to the fate of Egypt, but there was a long step between interest in an area and military occupation. Palmerston, who could hardly be accused of indifference to British interests, never wished for the occupation of Egypt. 'We do not want Egypt', he said in a famous passage 'or wish it for ourselves, any more than any rational man with an estate in the north of England and a residence in the south would have wished to possess the inns on the north road. All he could want would have been that the inns should be well-kept, always accessible, and furnishing him, when he came, with mutton-chops and post-horses' (71). Put less picturesquely, this is the 'informal' influence which Professors Robinson and Gallagher (96) contend was the British ideal in dealing with Africa (and many other parts of the world) in the nineteenth century. The difficulty was that, in British eyes, Egypt was ceasing to be 'well-kept' and 'always accessible' in the 1880s.

Mehemet Ali had died in 1849. Neither of his immediate successors, Abbas or Said, showed any great ability, but Said took a number of decisions of critical importance for the future of Egypt. Above all, he gave Ferdinand de Lesseps permission to go ahead with the building of the Suez Canal on terms very unfavourable to Egypt. The Canal was not in itself likely to be to Egypt's advantage since it would kill the lucrative 'overland' traffic. Nevertheless, Said agreed to take up 45 per cent of the shares in de Lesseps's company, to lease the land de Lesseps required, and to provide labour by an extension of the *corveé*-system, which compelled the Egyptian fellah (or peasant) to work for the government for a period each year on projects such as irrigation. Said took another decision which was to have unforeseen results. He promoted a number of native Egyptians, including a certain Ahmed Arabi, to the rank of colonel in the army.

When Said died in 1863, Egypt appeared tranquil and prosperous enough, although Said had had to raise a modest loan of rather over £3 million from Frühling and Goschen. Said was succeeded by his nephew Ismail, who has always attracted both critics and defenders. During his reign from 1863 to 1879 Egypt's foreign debt increased from £3 million to over £100 million. Some dismissed him as a mere irresponsible spendthrift but as the British cabinet minister, Stephen Cave, who investigated the situation in 1876 demonstrated [doc. 7] the truth was much more complex than that. A contemporary journalist was almost certainly right when he observed that Ismail had tried by diplomatic and financial means to accomplish what his predecessor, Mehemet Ali, had tried unsuccessfully to do by the sword, to transform Egypt into a powerful state, practically independent of the Sultan (66). He employed American officers, redundant after the Civil War, to pacify the Sudan, conquered by Mehemet Ali. He spent great sums in Constantinople to alter the normal Islamic law of succession so that he might be succeeded by his son, Tewfik, instead of by his brother and dangerous political rival, Halim. But a high proportion of his expenditure was accounted for by his attempts to turn Egypt into a 'modern' country. In some ways he was unlucky. There was an enormous boom in Egyptian cotton at the beginning of his reign because of the American Civil War. But the bubble burst as soon as the war ended. Ismail turned to sugar production to replace cotton, but some bad planning mistakes were made, refineries, for example, being sited in the wrong places. Nevertheless as Stephen Cave pointed out [doc. 7] worse mistakes were made during the English industrial revolution, but, whereas England could afford such mistakes, Egypt could not.

All the evidence is that Egypt's fundamental economy was sound enough. During the fifteen years of Ismail's reign her exports boomed. The cultivable area of Egypt increased by one-third, largely thanks to the new irrigation canals Ismail had built. Over 1,000 miles of railways were built: proportionately Egypt had more miles of railway than Austria or Spain. Alexandria was steadily transformed into a great Mediterranean port (66). The trouble was that Egypt did not have the capital to undertake these works herself. At first Ismail had no difficulty in raising capital in Europe; rather the contrary, for the low interest rates prevailing in Europe (at one time Bank Rate in Britain fell to 2 per cent) meant that investors were glad to consider loans to Egypt at a nominal rate of 7 per cent. He raised his first loan in 1864, intending to clear off the debt left by Said and use the surplus for public works. Thereafter loan followed loan at almost annual intervals. The amount actually received by the Egyptian treasury, after the expense of raising the loan in Europe, was often far less than the nominal amount. One observer calculated that the Egyptian treasury only received £35 million from five loans with a nominal value of over £55 million. Since interest was calculated on the nominal value this raised apparent rates of about 7 per cent to over 20 per cent in some cases. It was said that by 1875, having repaid over £29 million in interest and a sinking fund (on the £35 million actually received), the Egyptian government still owed over £46 million. Plainly, financially, Ismail was having to run to stand still. Moreover, whereas the earlier loans had been raised from highly respectable banking firms like Frühling and Goschen and Oppenheim and Company, Ismail was eventually reduced to desperate expedients of either accepting short term loans from very dubious financial groups, mainly French, or issuing 'treasury bonds' to cover debts immediately due (25, 66, 98).

By 1875 bankruptcy was staring him in the face. It was in these circumstances that Benjamin Disraeli, learning privately that Ismail was considering selling his Suez Canal shares to a French group, carried out his great *coup*, with the help of the Rothschilds, and bought the shares for the British government. Disraeli's hyperbolic phrase to the Queen, 'You have it [the Canal] Madam', was, of course, untrue. He had only secured 45 per cent of the shares and since Ismail had mortgaged the interest on these at an earlier stage in his financial embarrassment, they did not even carry voting rights. Nevertheless the whole transaction entered into the mythology of British imperialism. Like Stanley's meeting with Livingstone, it is one of the few episodes still remembered by the proverbial 'man on the top of the Clapham omnibus'. The British public, and perhaps some British politicians, became convinced that, in some peculiar sense, the Suez Canal was 'theirs' (24).

The following year Ismail asked for the assistance of two British Treasury officials to help him to sort out his finances. Instead Disraeli despatched his Paymaster General, Stephen Cave, to investigate the situation. There were some, unproven, suspicions that this was intended as a prelude to a British seizure of Egypt. If any such thought did pass through Disraeli's mind, the inevitable international complications provided a sufficient deterrent. Cave reported that the Egyptian situation was far from hopeless, but he did recommend the introduction of a stronger European element, which he regarded as both more efficient and less corrupt [doc. 7].

Cave's mission was followed by that of Goschen and Joubert. Joubert officially represented the French government, Goschen technically represented only a consortium of British bondholders. Goschen was a member of the banking firm which had raised the original loans for Said and Ismail — indeed, he said that this was why he felt under an obligation to undertake the mission — but he had personally renounced any financial interest some time before. Goschen and Joubert produced an elaborate scheme to bring some order to the Egyptian finances. There were to be two high officials, an Englishman to be Controller-General of the Revenue, and a Frenchman to be Controller-General of the Expenditure. They were to ensure that certain revenues which had been assigned to the servicing of the foreign debts were paid over to a Commission of the Public Debt, consisting of representatives of the bondholders. Once again, the French government had no objection to appearing as a principal in the transaction and appointed a representative on the Debt Commission. The British government, adhering to the traditional view that they would not accept responsibility for private investments made abroad by British citizens, refused an official nomination, but privately agreed that Evelyn Baring, later Lord Cromer, who had recently been acting as private secretary to Lord Northbrook, the Viceroy of India, should act for the British bondholders. Baring was a member of the great banking family of that name, although he had himself been a soldier and had no previous financial experience **(30).**

The Anglo-French 'Dual' financial control lasted (apart from the short abortive experiment of the 'European Ministry' in 1878-79) until the British occupation in 1882. It had considerable success in reducing the Egyptian finances to order. In 1880 the Law of Liquidation was agreed to, which had the effect of dividing the revenues of Egypt into two parts. The 'assigned revenues', such as the receipts of the railway, telegraph and customs departments and the port dues of Alexandria, were to be used to pay the charges on the foreign loans, with the interest on these now fixed more modestly at 4 or 5 per cent. The 'non-assigned' revenues, in effect all the rest, were to be used for the ordinary administrative purposes of the Egyptian government. If, however, the assigned revenues proved insufficient, the loan charges were to be the first charges on the non-assigned revenues, but if there was a surplus in the assigned revenues, this was not to be transferred to the administration but used to pay off the loans more quickly **(28, 30).** The basic health of the Egyptian economy meant that these charges were not crippling but, before the Dual Control began to work, the ordinary Egyptian had been reduced to straits of great misery. His plight was aggravated by the natural disaster of a 'low Nile' in 1876 and 1877 with resultant bad harvests. Egyptian methods of tax collection had always been brutal and the peasants fell into the hands of moneylenders, while in Upper Egypt hundreds actually starved to death. Politically more dangerous for the government was the disaffection in the army, whose pay was in arrears. The Egyptian officers were also discontented because Ismail had not continued Said's policy of promoting them rather than Turks (25, 30, 68).

The first army mutiny, that of February 1879, was almost certainly arranged by Ismail himself to get rid of the 'European ministry', but the soldiers quickly learnt their power (30). In June 1879 Ismail was deposed by his overlord, the Sultan, acting under German pressure. Lord Salisbury suspected that Bismarck was persuaded to take this action by Bleichroder and the German bankers who were angered by the neglect of German interests in Egypt (26). Historians have suspected the same but the matter remains unproven. Ismail was succeeded by his son Tewfik. Tewfik was acceptable to the powers because he was believed to be much more amenable to influence than Ismail. The powers soon had every reason to regret placing a weak man in such a crucial position.

Most historians have come to accept that what developed in Egypt in the late 1870s and early 1880s was a genuine national movement. Lord Cromer, who was virtually governor of Egypt from 1883 to 1907, eventually reached that conclusion himself (30, 96, 72). For many British Liberals, however, the situation was genuinely obscured by the prominent role of the Egyptian army [doc. 8]. Nevertheless, at first the British government was not altogether unsympathetic. Lord Granville, the Foreign Secretary, wrote a despatch in November 1881 at the request of Sir Edward Malet, the British Consul-General in Egypt (he had the title of 'consul-general', not 'ambassador', because Egypt, being part of the Ottoman empire, was not a sovereign state) expressing cautious approval of the reformers. This policy was reversed, at least in Egyptian eyes, by the Anglo-French Joint Note of 8 January 1882. On the face of it this was a restrained document simply expressing support for the Khedive against anyone who might disturb the peace. The British government meant that and no more, but it was Gambetta's government in Paris which had been the initiator of the Note, and the Egyptians immediately linked it with the French invasion of Tunis the previous year and feared that it was the prelude to intervention. There is little doubt that Gambetta was moved by his desire to protect the interests of the French bondholders. Gladstone's government, on the other hand, was deeply embarrassed by an association with the bondholders (35, 30).

Lord Cromer said later that the Note was like lighting a candle in a mine full of fire damp (30). From then on Britain and France on the one hand, and the Egyptian national movement on the other, were on a collision course. Possibly a confrontation could have been avoided if there had been a sufficient statesman in any of the three countries principally concerned. There was not. In France Freycinet replaced Gambetta and allowed matters to drift. In Britain, Lord Granville was elderly and indecisive. The Prime Minister, Gladstone, regarded Egypt as an irritating distraction from his real business at home and in Ireland. In Egypt Tewfik, in the aftermath of the excitement about the Joint Note, allowed the ministry of Cherif Pasha to retire. Opinions of Cherif differ, but in British eyes the educated and polished Cherif represented a moderate and comprehensible reform movement [doc. 8a]. They felt much less able to get on with his successor, Mahmoud Pasha Sami, an avowed nationalist, who included in his cabinet Arabi Pasha, one of the leaders of the army 'mutinies' of February and September 1881.

The situation deteriorated rapidly. Sir Edward Malet sent home somewhat alarmist reports of the danger to European lives and property in Egypt. Late in May Britain and France sent a small squadron of warships to Alexandria, nominally to evacuate refugees, but in part to try to overawe the Egyptians and ensure that there would be no violent outbreaks — a tactic that had occasionally worked in other parts of the world. This time, however, it did not. On Sunday, 11 June 1882, there was a violent riot in Alexandria in which about fifty Europeans, including an officer and two sailors from the British fleet, were killed. The British government believed, almost certainly wrongly, that Arabi Pasha and the nationalists, had been behind the riot. Negotiations between the two sides became virtually impossible. A month later, on 11 July, the British fleet bombarded the fortifications which were in process of erection at Alexandria. Militarily there was a valid excuse for doing so — work had been resumed after the Egyptians had promised it would stop — but even Gladstone in the House of Commons admitted that there was an element of revenge in the action, for he feared that, if the massacre of 11 June remained unavenged, all the scattered British communities in distant places would be at a risk (35, 43, 80).

After the bombardment of 11 July there was no real alternative to military intervention. Arabi's army camped outside Alexandria and cut off water supplies to the town. The Suez Canal was probably in real danger — certainly the British government believed it to be so. They now felt that the Canal would only be safe if 'anarchy' were put down in Cairo. The Quaker John Bright had resigned from the cabinet rather than agree to the bombardment, arguing that if it would endanger the Canal it had better not be undertaken. But no one went with him. Gladstone and his colleagues were puzzled and unhappy but committed (96).

They still hoped to avoid a unilateral intervention. Technically the Sultan, as suzerain, had the strongest legal right to intervene and, despite the embarrassment of calling on the 'abominable' Turk after Gladstone's denunciation of the 'Bulgarian Horrors' four years earlier, the British tried to persuade him to act. The Sultan, however, had no intention of being the cat's paw of Britain and France and determinedly procrastinated. Gladstone hoped that Britain and France might intervene jointly as the 'mandatories' of Europe, preserving his ideal of the Concert of Europe acting on the Eastern Question (35, 76). The Freycinet government, however, failed to secure the necessary vote of credit in the Chambers at the end of July and fell. The British even tried to secure a joint intervention with Italy. But the most influential man in Europe was the German Chancellor, Otto von Bismarck. Germany, Austria and Italy kept closely in step (this was the year of the signing of the Triple Alliance). Privately, Bismarck encouraged Britain to intervene swiftly, if necessary alone. Possibly he hoped for a diplomatic breach between England and France: possibly he simply hoped to end this dangerous reopening of the Eastern Question as quickly as possible [docs 9a-c] (35, 43).

The British military intervention in August 1882, nominally undertaken with the approval of Tewfik against a rebellious army, was a textbook success. Sir Garnet Wolseley, who had done all the previous contingency planning at the War Office (with the help of the Under Secretary, Henry Campbell-Bannerman), commanded the expedition. After a feint at Aboukir, he made straight for the Canal. It was captured in three days. The Egyptian army was finally defeated at Tel-el-Kebir on 13 September 1882. Arabi and some of his associates were put on trial and eventually exiled to Ceylon.

The Gladstone government had every intention of withdrawing their forces immediately Arabi had been defeated, but they soon found that government had apparently collapsed in Egypt. Withdrawal was not easy. Gladstone himself said bitterly, 'We have done our Egyptian business, and we are an Egyptian government' (80).

Moreover, the Sudan had risen under its own leader, the Mahdi, and was threatening the security of Egypt proper. The British government put pressure on the Egyptians to cut their losses and evacuate the Sudan. General Gordon, who had been Governor of the Sudan for a time under Ismail and was believed still to have a fund of goodwill among the Sudanese where he had tried to suppress the slave trade, was sent to carry out the evacuation. Gordon's name, however, was no match for the magic of the Mahdi. Gordon was a strange and wilful man; possibly he even had, as Anthony Nutting suggests, a subconscious desire for martyrdom. His death at Khartoum in January 1885 certainly made him a martyr in the eyes of the British people. The *History of the*

Times suggests that the *Times's* correspondent, Frank le Poer Power (who was himself killed trying to get a message from Gordon to Kitchener), highlighted Gordon for the British public, much as William Russell highlighted Florence Nightingale during the Crimean War. Whatever the mechanics by which some incidents in history become memorable and others, equally dramatic, do not, Gordon at Khartoum became another of the great legends of British imperialism. The idea of 'avenging Gordon' was immensely popular in some quarters [**doc. 10**] **(50, 84)**.

But the tragedy also started a torrent of criticism about the whole British involvement in Egypt. This had been strangely muted until then. Only a few independents, like Frederic Harrison, had suggested that the British invasion of 1882 had been a complete reversal of the whole 'Midlothian' programme of non-intervention and the rights of small nations on which Gladstone had fought the 1880 election [**doc. 8c**]. Most of the critics had been dissident conservatives, like the eccentric Wilfrid Scawen Blunt, with his dreams of a resurgent pan-Arab empire, independent of Constantinople. Blunt was closely in touch with the Egyptian nationalists and, such were the workings of the British political system at this time, that he was able, through his personal friendship with Edward Hamilton, Gladstone's private secretary, to get the ear of Gladstone himself and come very close to persuading Gladstone that he had misunderstood the whole Egyptian situation **(25)**. The campaign was later taken up by Lord Randolph Churchill, who had been ill in 1882, but who in 1883 was one of the most strenuous denouncers of the whole intervention as a 'bondholders' war' [**doc. 8d**]. But liberal opinion in general was held for a time in uneasy silence by Gladstone's own great prestige.

When the denunciation began it lasted for a generation. Egypt came to be regarded as the classical case of financial imperialism. Capitalists invested in foreign countries, sometimes on usurious terms, then demanded the protection of their government, by military force if necessary **(98, 112, 117)**. Against this it has been argued that Britain intervened in Egypt for strategic reasons, because of the vital importance of the Suez Canal **(96)**. But for the Canal, British investors would have been told, as they had been told in other cases, that risky foreign speculations were their responsibility, not the government's **(124)**. There is little doubt that Gladstone's government had no intention of fighting a bondholders' war. But the situation is not quite so simple as that. The British government intervened in August 1882 because they believed, rightly or wrongly, that the Suez Canal was in immediate danger. But the Canal would never have been in any sort of danger but for the situation which had developed in Cairo and Alexandria, and it is more difficult to argue that that was not directly connected with the foreign financial and political pressures to which Egypt had been subjected for the previous twenty years.

The British occupation of Egypt ended Anglo-French understanding there and caused difficulties in the relations between the two countries until the Agreements of 1904. The French were irritated, not so much by the actual intervention, from which they realised they had withdrawn by their own act, but by the subsequent British actions in remaining in Egypt and ending the Anglo-French Dual Control as part of their general 'tidying up' of the tangled Egyptian situation. It has been contended by some historians, and strenuously denied by others, that the Anglo-French estrangement over Egypt had repercussions all over Africa, that indeed it was the trigger that began an unexpected and unintended chain reaction that resulted in the partition of tropical Africa among the European great powers (**96, 139, 149**).

The Egyptian case attracted immense attention from later imperial theorists. To some, J. A. Hobson among them, it went far to prove that the whole imperialist movement was financial in origin, a fraud on the whole nation by a sectional interest (**117**). If this were the case then the insights gained from an analysis of the Egyptian example would be generally applicable and would provide a general theory of imperialism. Some writers have held that that was so. Others, however, have questioned it, pointing out that the financial motives that are so obvious in Egypt are by no means so easily proven in tropical Africa (**133**). If the latter school of thought is correct, Egypt must be treated as a special case, a unique combination of strategic and financial interests, not a general explanation of imperialism, and other cases must be investigated to see what pattern, if any, emerges from them.

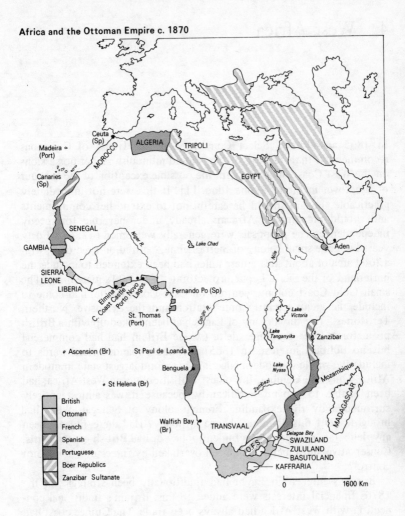

Africa and the Ottoman Empire c. 1870

Madeira ○ (Port)

Canaries (Sp)

Ceuta (Sp)

MOROCCO

ALGERIA

TRIPOLI

EGYPT

SENEGAL

GAMBIA

SIERRA LEONE

LIBERIA

Niger R.

Lake Chad

Aden

Elmina C. Coast Castle Porto Novo Lagos

Fernando Po (Sp)

St. Thomas (Port)

Congo R.

Lake Victoria

Lake Tanganyika

Zanzibar

○ Ascension (Br)

St Paul de Loanda

Benguela

Lake Nyasa

Mozambique

○ St Helena (Br)

Zambezi

MADAGASCAR

Walfish Bay (Br)

TRANSVAAL

Delagoa Bay

SWAZILAND

O.F.S.

ZULULAND

BASUTOLAND

KAFFRARIA

British
Ottoman
French
Spanish
Portuguese
Boer Republics
Zanzibar Sultanate

0   1600 Km

45

4 West Africa

In 1865 an all-party Select Committee of the House of Commons recommended that, ideally, Britain should relinquish all her possessions on the West Coast of Africa with the possible exception of the harbour of Freetown in Sierra Leone [doc. 11]. If this were not immediately practicable, Britain should be careful not to extend her commitments and should prepare the Africans already under her rule for speedy independence. The proposals were generally welcomed (47, 67). Forty years later the small colony of Sierra Leone, centred on Freetown, with a total area of about 250 square miles had been extended to include the hinterland of the Sierra Leone protectorate of 27,000 square miles. The small Gold Coast colony, centred on Cape Coast Castle, had come to include the great Ashanti Confederation and the extensive 'Northern Territories'. The tiny colony of Lagos had been linked up with a British protectorate over the Niger delta (where Britain had had commercial but no political interests in 1865) and had expanded northwards to include the whole of modern Nigeria, the second largest state in modern Africa. Only the Gambia, the oldest British colony in West Africa, had been unable to expand significantly, because it was almost entirely surrounded by the expanding French colony of Senegal. What had brought about this dramatic change in policy? Had there, indeed, been any deliberate change of government policy or had British governments, Conservative and Liberal alike, been overtaken by forces they could not control?

Britain's interest in Egypt had traditionally been strategic; in the 1870s financial interests were added to this. Britain's traditional connection with West Africa had always been trade. The Guinea coast had been one corner of the important 'triangular trade' with the West Indies (see Chapter 1). When the slave trade was forbidden in 1807, new trades slowly grew up to replace it. The most important of these was the trade in palm oil carried on between British merchants, mainly from Liverpool, and the chiefs of the Niger delta, the so-called, 'Oil Rivers' (57). In return for the oil the British merchants supplied cheap textiles, mainly from Manchester, some hardware from Sheffield and Birmingham, firearms also from Birmingham, and spirits mostly imported from Holland. The trade of the Oil Rivers was opened up by British capital and enterprise, as indignant merchants were later to remind their government [doc. 12], and for many years Britain was alone in the field. Britain, however, undertook no formal political responsibilities in the Niger delta during the first three-quarters of the century. Only in 1849 did they appoint a British consul 'for the Bights of Benin and Biafra'. This was John Beecroft, sailor, explorer, merchant and antislavery crusader. Beecroft was a very remarkable man; Professor Dike calls him 'something of an institution in the Bight of Biafra'. He had no authority except that of an ordinary consul, but, such was the respect he commanded among Europeans and Africans, that he became a kind of general arbiter. Dike goes on so far as to conclude:

> In time Africans came to look on the British Consul as the *de facto* Governor of the Bights of Benin and Biafra. This position of power which Beecroft won for himself passed on to his successors and enabled Britain to enjoy the authority of a protecting power before the Berlin West Africa Conference had legalised that status in international diplomacy (32).

With 'moral suasion' (96) so satisfactorily established on that part of the Guinea Coast, the British government had no desire for any more costly or demanding kind of influence there, unless or until they should be directly challenged.

The challenge in fact came first in other areas. The British had long maintained a few forts in the region of Cape Coast on the Gold Coast. In 1850 and 1872 respectively they bought the remaining Danish and Dutch forts in the region. Although this might seem strange at a time when the British were wondering whether it was worth maintaining their presence on the Gold Coast at all, the explanation is that they hoped that the additional stations might make the colony financially self-sufficient. British governments in the middle of the nineteenth century had no objections to mercantile stations in distant places so long as they were neither a political nor a financial liability. The Gold Coast, however, soon came to be both. British commercial relations were with the Fanti people on the coast, but the Fanti enjoyed very precarious relations with their powerful inland neighbours, the Ashanti Confederation. The Ashanti Confederation, which had originally been formed by a few small tribes to defend themselves against aggressive neighbours, had grown on the profits of the slave trade into one of the strongest states in West Africa. The head of the Confederation, the Asantehene, had his capital at Kumasi and the symbol of his authority was the famous 'golden stool' which, legend said, had come straight from

47

heaven. Throughout the nineteenth century the Ashanti were anxious to extend their authority to the coast, and after 1807 they were resentful of the British influence which was used against their slaving activities. The first serious clash occurred in the 1820s. In 1823 they defeated Sir Charles McCarthy and a small British army. (McCarthy was killed and his skull seized as a trophy and made into a drinking cup.) The British defeated the Ashanti in 1826 but made no attempt to penetrate inland. After 1830 a young army officer, George Maclean, established an influence on the Gold Coast similar to that which Beecroft had achieved in the Oil Rivers, and in 1844 the British government signed treaties with a number of Fanti chiefs which entitled them to some degree of British protection. The situation again became critical in 1863 when the British Governor refused to return a fugitive slave to the Ashanti. The Ashanti invaded the 'protectorate'. The campaign became a stalemate but there was a significant number of British casualties. Revulsion against the futility of the Ashanti War formed the background to the Report of the Select Committee quoted at the beginning of this chapter.

Yet another Ashanti War broke out in 1873. The immediate cause was another Ashanti invasion of the protectorate provoked by the transfer of the Dutch possessions (the Dutch had been on good terms with the Ashanti) to their enemies, the British. This war attracted a good deal more publicity than its predecessors. It was conducted with vigour and success by one of the ablest men in the British army, Garnet Wolseley, who defeated the Ashanti and temporarily occupied their capital. It was reported by a remarkable band of war correspondents, including H. M. Stanley, G. A. Henty and Winwood Reade. After Wolseley's victory, Disraeli's government decided in July 1874 to constitute the vague Fanti protectorate into a crown colony. At first glance this might appear to be an example of the more 'forward' policy of Disraeli's new conservative administration, but Professor McIntyre demonstrates that all the critical decisions had been taken at the end of the previous Liberal administration, when Gladstone was still prime minister and Lord Kimberley, colonial secretary (**67**). The policy of the 1865 committee, the so-called 'Cardwell policy' (Cardwell had been a leading member of the committee), had been virtually abandoned. On the Gold Coast the challenge had come from an African power, but this was unusual in the situation that was now developing on the West Coast.

In the 1850s the French colony of Senegal began to expand in area under the vigorous leadership of General Faidherbe, who first became its governor in 1854. Senegal expanded until it virtually engulfed the old British colony of the Gambia. The Gambia was of little real use to Britain, but to the French it now began to assume some importance as a possible trade route. The idea of exchanging the Gambia for some other part of West Africa more immediately valuable to the British was first mooted in 1861. It was seriously discussed in 1865-66 and on several occasions in the 1870s but, by now, a remarkably powerful 'Gambia lobby' had emerged, partly commercial, partly missionary, which was strongly opposed to any cession of British territory there (47). The project was to be revived at intervals – it was discussed as late as the Anglo-French agreements of 1904 – but the idea of ceding territory once British had now become quite repugnant. The British attitude to colonies was very slowly but surely changing.

Two new factors entered into the situation in the late 1870s. One was a great increase in French interest in the area, partly military, partly commercial. The other was a challenge by a new group of British merchants to the Liverpool merchants who had so long traded with the chiefs of the Niger Delta. These chiefs were only middlemen. The palm oil in which they traded was produced further up the Niger. It occurred to some British traders that it might be profitable to bypass them and to deal directly with the primary producers on the middle Niger. The moving spirit in this was a Manxman, George Taubman Goldie [**docs 12a, 15**] **(36)**. Goldie, originally an officer in the Royal Engineers, had been left some shares in a small company trading on the Niger by an uncle. He decided to go out to the Niger and assess the situation for himself. In 1879 he persuaded a number of small companies to join together in what was originally known as the United African Company. In 1882 this was changed into the National African Company. Goldie had considerable luck in persuading a South Wales industrialist, Lord Aberdare, who was also President of the Royal Geographical Society and a former Liberal Home Secretary, to become Chairman of the new company. Aberdare, although he had left high political office for good in 1874, still had the ear of Gladstone and of Lord Granville, the Foreign Secretary, 1880-85, in a way in which no outsider could have had. Goldie also secured the support of James Hutton, a Manchester M.P. and President of the Manchester Chamber of Commerce, 1884-85. Hutton was an extremely influential man who had a finger in most African pies at this time [**docs 12c, 17**]. Goldie needed all the support he could get, for his plans for the Niger were far-reaching. In 1881 the British government had revived the old device of a Royal Chartered Company for the North Borneo Company. This once-favoured form of organisation (the great East India Company was the classic example) had been generally regarded as obsolete since 1857, but now Goldie began to study the precedents with interest. Nevertheless, it is unlikely that the British Government would have regarded the new ambitions of the Niger traders very sympathetically but for the sudden challenge from France in the area.

Faidherbe had finally left Senegal in 1865 and his ambitious plans went into cold storage. In 1871 Napoleon III was defeated at Sedan and the Second Empire collapsed. Most Frenchmen under the Third Republic had their eyes fixed on the 'blue line of the Vosges' and the lost provinces of Alsace and Lorraine, but a powerful lobby eventually developed which saw colonial success as some measure of compensation for defeat in Europe and a new source of both prestige and economic strength. The French statesman most usually associated with this is Jules Ferry, who was responsible for the French forward moves in both Tunis and Indo-China in the early 1880s, but Dr Kanya-Forstner shows that Charles Freycinet, who is usually remembered for his weak policy on Egypt, had ambitious plans for West Africa. He was ably supported by Admiral Jauréguiberry, a former Governor of Senegal who became Minister of Marine in February 1879. These plans turned on building a great railway network (Freycinet was himself a former railway engineer) which would link Senegal, Algeria and the Upper Niger. (**58, 114, 140, 141**).

The British merchants on the Lower and Middle Niger were generally resigned to the fact that the Upper Niger was destined to pass into the French sphere, and in 1883 Goldie and Aberdare urged the British government to strike a bargain with France which would leave the river below Timbuktu under British influence. The traders were more alarmed by the new French challenge which seemed to be being mounted to British interests all round the coast from Sierra Leone to the Congo. To the north of Sierra Leone, the disputed area concerned what were then generally called the Southern Rivers, which Sierra Leone believed to be within its sphere of influence but which the French saw as a possible outlet for their Soudanese trade. Between 1877 and 1882, when an agreement was finally signed, the British and French continually manoeuvred for position in the region. On the stretch of coast between the Gold Coast and Lagos, the French revived an old protectorate over Porto Novo in 1883. Porto Novo had complicated relations with the powerful inland state of Dahomey (both were successor states of the once-important state of Ardra). In 1861 Britain annexed Lagos, which was one of the last surviving slaving centres on the coast, most of its victims being prisoners of war from the disintegrating Yoruba empire in what later became western Nigeria. As part of the same sequence of events the French had briefly exercised a protectorate over Porto Novo in 1863-65 (**47**). Professors Robinson and Gallagher in their *Africa and the Victorians* (**96**) put forward the hypothesis that the French resumption of the protectorate in 1883 was a deliberate tit-for-tat for the British occupation of Egypt. Dr Newbury, however, has shown beyond reasonable doubt that the French decision had been taken before the British invasion of Egypt (**139**). Nevertheless, it does seem that the Porto Novo protectorate was a deliberate French attempt to prevent the British from securing an unbroken sphere of influence on the coast from Lagos to the Gold Coast. Robinson and Gallagher also suggested that the French probing of the British position on the Niger was another manifestation of the breakdown of the unspoken 'gentleman's agreement' which, they posited, had restrained the British and the French from encroaching upon each other's spheres in West Africa but which was abandoned after the Egyptian fiasco. Again, however, the balance of the evidence seems to be clearly that the reasons for the French action are to be found in West Africa. The French were anxious, if possible, to secure a route from the Bight of Benin to the Upper Niger which *bypassed*, not challenged, the existing British influence in the Niger Delta (**139**). Nevertheless, the British did feel challenged [doc. 12].

Two French companies, the Compagnie Française de l'Afrique Équatoriale and the Compagnie du Sénégal et de la Côte Occidentale de l'Afrique, began operating on the Niger. The British identified as their most formidable opponent a certain Lieutenant Mattei, a man not unlike Goldie himself, an army officer who had obtained leave to come to the coast. The French gave Mattei a consular appointment and the British believed, wrongly in fact, that the French government was giving Mattei substantial financial backing. Mattei tried to conclude a treaty with the chiefs at Bonny which, in the opinion of local observers, would have amounted to a French protectorate. The British traders also became alarmed by the activities of French warships on the coast and eventually induced the (usually rather sceptical) British Admiralty to call for urgent reports. The National African Company, however, decided, correctly, that its best hope was to buy out its potential rivals. After undercutting the French prices, at considerable cost to its own profits, it induced the French to sell out in 1884. Lord Granville, hardly the most jingoistic of English Foreign Secretaries, was sufficiently carried away to write 'Hurrah' on the back of the letter informing him of this (**36, 139, 149**).

The new danger to British trade on the Niger seemed likely to be paralleled on the Congo. While Britain had fewer commercial interests on the Congo where the principal traders were Dutch (**149**) than on the

Niger, a number of Liverpool firms had a foothold there [doc. 12b]. The Portuguese still had some shadowy claims to sovereignty at the mouth of the Congo, based on their old connection with the area. The British government, however, had consistently refused to recognise these, notably in a despatch from the then Foreign Secretary, Lord Clarendon, in 1853. The British reluctance to recognise Portuguese jurisdiction anywhere on the coast of Africa where it could avoid it was due to two considerations; first, the bad Portuguese record in tolerating the continuance of the slave trade; and secondly, the high tariffs which the Portuguese habitually charged on foreign goods. The situation, however, rapidly changed in the early 1880s (21).

A new factor appeared with the sudden entry on to the scene of Leopold II, King of the Belgians. Leopold had dreamed of a colonial empire since he had been Crown Prince in the 1860s. Central Africa was not his first choice but his earlier schemes came to nothing and when first Lovett Cameron [doc. 3] and then H. M. Stanley returned with glowing tales of the possibilities of the Congo Basin, which the British government ignored, Leopold acted quickly. He had little or no backing from the Belgian Parliament and he played a remarkable lone hand. In 1876 he invited an extremely distinguished array of geographers and explorers to Brussels to a Conference. There were precedents, notably the Paris Conference of 1875, but Leopold had made exceptionally careful preparations. As he intended, the result of the Conference was the setting up of the Association Internationale Africaine (A.I.A.) for the suppression of the slave trade and the opening up of Central Africa, with Leopold as President and prestigious 'national committees' – the chairman of the British committee was the Prince of Wales. The British government initially seems to have accepted that Leopold's motives were entirely scientific and humanitarian. It was only in 1884 that strange private reports began to filter into the Foreign Office of questionable activities in the Congo (87). Different opinions about Leopold's sincerity are possible. The Congo eventually provided the greatest scandal of the whole colonial era in Africa, when E. D. Morel and others revealed to the world the cruel exploitation which had accompanied the development of the rubber industry there (79). It could be that Leopold was genuinely ignorant of the excesses of his dubious agents there, but he was one of the few men to make a great personal fortune out of Africa in this period (22), and most men perhaps came to agree with Lord Rosebery, who once said that he would be better able to believe in Leopold's sincerity if he looked less like Fagin[1]. Some historians have contended that it was Leopold's

[1] The *Rosebery Papers*, Box 109 (National Library of Scotland).

activities, more than any other single factor, which set off the 'Scramble' in West Africa (10, 149). The International Association began to conclude treaties with African chiefs in the Congo. It now seems to be established that the initial treaties were commercial ones, but that when Leopold revealed them to the world in 1884 he represented them as political treaties, transferring sovereignty (149). The deception was probably attributable to Leopold's fear, by 1884, of French competition.

The French had a colony, Gabon, to the north of the mouth of the Congo, founded in 1841. Some Frenchmen believed that the way to tap the great potential wealth of the Congo Basin was not by the river Congo itself, which was badly obstructed by rapids near its mouth, but by the river Ogoué which would channel the trade into Gabon. One of the men who believed this was the French explorer, Savorgnan de Brazza. Nominally employed by the French 'national committee', which had been set up in 1876, he undertook an expedition up the Ogoué to the vicinity of Stanley Pool. Indeed the whole expedition became a sort of race with Stanley himself, now in the employ of Leopold. De Brazza concluded a series of treaties in October 1880 with an African chief he knew as the Makoko (a title not, as many supposed at the time, a proper name). These treaties purported to cede large territories to De Brazza as the representative of France, but they were vague and, legally, highly irregular. The French government's original reaction was to pigeon-hole them, much as the British government had done with some rather similar treaties which Lovett Cameron had concluded six years earlier. The Makoko treaty was, however, finally accepted as valid by the French government in November 1882. Indirectly this seems to have been the result of the Egyptian crisis. It was not that the French government saw the Makoko treaty as an attack on Britain – on the contrary they were still trying to conciliate Britain in the hope of saving something from the wreck in Egypt – but the French public, angered by the weak role their country had played in Egypt, was peculiarly susceptible to the powerful Press campaign that De Brazza and his associates now mounted in favour of a forward policy on the Congo. The government dared not resist (21, 149).

The British government was in turn alarmed by the new French interest. Since 1879 they had been engaged in often rather desultory negotiations with Portugal to settle certain colonial questions concerning Goa, Mozambique and the Congo. Those concerning the Congo were now taken up with renewed vigour and resulted in the Anglo-Portuguese treaty of February 1884, by which the British government recognised Portugal's ancient claims to jurisdiction over the mouth of the Congo. They also agreed, against their own better judgment, that the navigation of the Congo should be regulated by an Anglo-Portuguese commission — Britain would have preferred an international commission (21).

The treaty was signed but not yet ratified and there was an immediate outcry from commercial interests in Britain [doc. 12c]. The outcry was not entirely spontaneous. It was clearly organised from Manchester, mainly by James Hutton, who was himself in touch with Leopold of the Belgians[1]. But it gained widespread support. British merchants had lost none of their suspicions of Portuguese protectionist policies and the British government had demonstrably been careless in the terms they had negotiated. They had, for example, agreed that the new 'Mozambique tariff' should be applied to the Congo, believing it to be a liberal one, but had failed to notice that the duties levied under it on textiles were calculated by weight, not by value: $2\frac{3}{4}d$ to $4\frac{3}{4}d$ per pound on the high grade Indian textiles that made up most of Mozambique's imports was moderate; the same rate on the very cheap Manchester goods that went to the Congo would be the equivalent of about 30 per cent on the value and crippling. The government began to fear that they would be defeated in Parliament on the issue. They were not sorry to find a way to avoid ratification.

This was just as well because other European powers were angered by the prospect of a private Anglo-Portuguese settlement of what they regarded as an international question. In Germany, the Chancellor, Otto von Bismarck, saw the opportunity for a diplomatic coup. Alsace-Lorraine had made it impossible for Bismarck to effect a reconciliation with France after 1871, as he had done so successfully with Austria after 1866. Ideally, he would almost certainly have preferred a restoration of good relations with France. The French prime minister, Jules Ferry, was known to be interested in colonial questions. Bismarck, who was beginning to be interested in colonial questions himself and considered that he had reason to be annoyed with Britain for the latter's cavalier treatment of German claims (see below, p. 58), seized the chance to suggest to France that they might act together to put pressure on Britain over the Congo. The Franco-German colonial *entente* was shortlived — the Germans as the newcomers in the colonial field soon found that they had more in common with free trade Britain than with protectionist France — but while it lasted it had extremely important consequences (23, 31, 40, 104).

The French and the Germans persuaded the Portuguese to put the

---

[1] The evidence for this is in the *Mackinnon Papers* in the School of Oriental and African Studies in the University of London. Some of it is quoted in (21).

question of the Congo to an international conference of all the interested parties, including the United States of America. The conference was held in Berlin from November 1884 to February 1885, the main item on the agenda being the Congo, but the Niger and 'new occupations' of the coast of Africa were also discussed. It really laid down the rules under which the 'Scramble' for Africa was conducted during the next six years.

Britain's motive in concluding the Anglo-Portuguese treaty had been to prevent the French from securing a dominant position in the Congo and she was quite happy to see the question 'internationalised'. The settlement of the Congo by the Berlin Act of 1885 was unprecedented in international law. The provisions concerning the river itself, promising freedom of navigation for all, had some precedents in the very successful clauses of the Treaty of Vienna of 1815 concerning the international rivers of Europe. Gladstone himself had been very interested in this aspect and hoped that similar provisions might be applied to all international waterways, including the Suez Canal. But the Act went much further than this and laid down that in a vast area of Central Africa, the 'Conventional Basin' of the Congo, much larger than the geographical basin, there was to be freedom of commerce for all without discrimination of nationality. The Basin was also to be neutralised in time of war, and a number of humanitarian clauses tried to secure religious toleration and the protection of native rights and the end of the slave trade [doc. 14]. Most of these clauses became a dead letter. Administrative control of a large part of the area passed to Leopold's Congo Free State, which was recognised as a sovereign state by the leading powers during or after the Conference (21, 31).

The British government was not at first unwilling to consider the possibility of allowing the Conference to lay down similar conditions on the Niger to those proposed on the Congo, but more cautious counsels prevailed. They decided that Britain must appear at the Conference as '*the* Niger power'. Considering Britain's apparently weak diplomatic position at the beginning of the Conference, with Germany and France united to put pressure on her over the Congo, she emerged with remarkable success. The Congo settlement was not unacceptable to her. The Niger one was very favourable. Britain's predominant position on the Lower and Middle Niger was internationally recognised. In return Britain agreed to observe freedom of navigation on the Niger similar to that laid down on the Congo (31, 36).

It was the third 'basis' of the Conference negotiations, that regulating 'new occupations' on the coast of Africa and laying down the doctrine of 'effective occupation' [doc. 14], which in some ways caused the British government most anxiety. They wanted, and received, assurances that it would apply only to future, not to recent, acquisitions. The whole idea of establishing 'effective occupation' of an area was a departure from the traditional British policy of trying to secure only a degree of influence which would ensure that their interests were not discriminated against in favour of any other power. Other countries too were affected by these new definitions. The Berlin Conference was, perhaps, primarily a manoeuvre in European diplomacy with Bismarck using the Congo question as a pawn (31). It was called to settle only certain specified questions. The insistence on 'effective occupation' was probably only intended to abrogate Portugal's ancient but shadowy claims to half the coast line of Africa. But its consequences were far-reaching. Claims which had been left vague were now clearly defined, and the European powers felt compelled to assert their presence on the ground as never before.

Even before the Conference met, the British traders on the Niger had set out to consolidate their position. The National African Company, through its agent David MacIntosh, had begun to sign treaties with the local chiefs, purporting to transfer sovereign rights to the Company. When he saw them subsequently, the Lord Chancellor, Lord Selborne, could not conceal his scepticism. Would any body of men, he asked, sign away their rights for such vague benefits as the Company promised them? The treaties were mostly on printed forms and in English only, although they had supposedly been translated and explained to the signatories [doc. 15b]. There seems little doubt that the signatures (or, more usually, witnessed marks) were genuine enough, but it is likely that the chiefs thought that they were signing treaties of trade and amity, similar to others which had been concluded in the past, and had no suspicion of the very different construction which was about to be put upon such treaties by all the European powers (36).

Treaties with a commercial company, however, would have only a limited status in international law. The Niger traders were convinced that they must get government backing for their position. The argument went on for a long time in Gladstone's cabinet. The forces of the Colonial Office and the Treasury were firmly ranged against any extension of British responsibilities. The Foreign Office was divided in its counsels. Some permanent officials, like Thomas Villiers Lister, the assistant under-secretary with special responsibility for African affairs, became converts to the idea that Britain must act to protect British trade. The government tried, briefly, to put forward the doctrine that the traders who desired protection must be prepared to pay for it, for example, by paying for British consuls on the coast. The traders soon scotched that one. Hutton and Goldie told the Foreign Office, 'To keep France back is a national necessity.' Lord Aberdare demonstrated that British trade with the Niger was greater than with Greece or Japan, where the government paid for consular services without question. The Foreign Office acquiesced. In the last resort it acknowledged that the defence of British trade was a government responsibility [doc. 13] (36).

The British Consul at Fernando Po, Edward Hewett, was instructed to conclude treaties with the Niger chiefs which would virtually establish a British protectorate in the region. These treaties, concluded in the summer of 1884, were much more carefully explained to the signatories than were the Company's 'treaties' − in many instances the chiefs insisted on detailed changes in certain clauses[1]. They were an important factor in allowing Britain to appear at Berlin as 'the Niger power'. The Company, however, did its share by hastily extending its activities to the important tributary of the Niger, the Benue, to comply with the new ideas about 'effective occupations'. Almost immediately after the Conference in 1885 Britain was able to reach agreement with Germany about the British sphere of influence in the region and in June 1885 a formal notice was inserted in the *London Gazette* proclaiming a British protectorate. The British government was now faced with the problem of exercising its jurisdiction. Goldie was still ready with his suggestion of a Chartered Company. The matter was argued at length. The Liberal government fell in June 1885 and was succeeded by Lord Salisbury's first Conservative government, which held office until February 1886. It is interesting that there is no discernible difference in the attitude of the two parties to Goldie's proposals. The matter was settled eventually for the reasons which T. V. Lister had spelt out in a memorandum as early as January 1885. If the British government discharged its new responsibilities directly, it would have to face the expense of establishing a colonial government and a river fleet. The Company was on the spot with agents and steamers.

It is [said Lister] perfectly able and willing to discharge the duties of administration . . . and unless it should be considered necessary that this country should go to the great expense of setting up the machinery of Government upon the two rivers where the Company now rules supreme, there seems to be no other course open, and certainly no better one, than that of legalizing and affirming the position of the Company and placing the business of administration into its hands.

---

[1] This judgment is based on F.O. Confidential Prints 5021, 5063, *Granville Papers*, P.R.O. 30/29/270 (Public Record Office).

In 1886 the National African Company became the Royal Niger Company [**doc. 15a**]. So was born the first of the great African chartered companies by which Britain ruled vast tracts of Africa in the late nineteenth century (36).

The agreement of 1885 about the British sphere on the Lower Niger had been reached with Germany, not the old rival, France. This was symptomatic of a rapidly changing situation. Germany had now appeared as a major factor in Africa. The first Anglo-German clash had centred on the region between Cape Colony and the Portuguese colony of Angola, the region which subsequently became German South West Africa. In 1878 Britain had annexed a small station there, Walfisch Bay, but generally no one had previously paid much attention to this barren and unpromising stretch of coast line. The only resident Europeans were missionaries from the Barmen Rhine Society, who had originally gone to southern Africa under the auspices of the London Missionary Society. When the German government enquired, in February 1883, whether Britain claimed to exercise any jurisdiction in the area, the British thought that they were seeking protection for the missionaries and returned a polite but evasive reply. It only very slowly dawned on the British that the Germans, who had previously insisted that they had no colonial interests in Africa, wanted to take control of the region themselves. In fact, the Germans may have only reached that conclusion themselves in the course of the negotiations (40). The German government too was under pressure from its traders to protect their overseas interests. A certain Herr Lüderitz, who had previously been associated with several of his countrymen in ambitious plans for the Transvaal, had set up a trading station at Angra Pequeña near Walfisch Bay in April 1883. The British government had no strong objection to a German presence there, since so far Britain had had no significant colonial quarrels with Germany. But there was another party to the question. Cape Colony had finally attained 'responsible government' in 1872, in effect complete internal autonomy. The Cape colonists were naturally very interested in what happened on their northern frontier. The British government felt compelled to consult them. The consultation involved long delays, and the Germans, who had little understanding of or sympathy with the very complex constitutional relationships that were evolving within the British empire, regarded it as a mere time wasting device on the part of the British. The Cape government came out very strongly in favour of refusing to recognise the presence of any other power between the Cape and Angola. The British government, however, was exasperated by what they saw as the growing tendency of their colonies (the Australians felt much as the South

Africans did about their neighbouring territories) to proclaim a 'kind of Monroe doctrine' over their region – a Monroe doctrine which the British navy and therefore the British taxpayer, would be compelled to uphold. When the German government announced in April 1884 that they would protect Lüderitz's settlement and when it was made clear later in the summer of 1884 that this was a territorial and not merely a 'consular' form of protection, the British government acquiesced without many misgivings, although they were irritated by what they saw as Germany's unnecessarily discourteous treatment of a traditionally friendly power (**23**, **40**, **104**).

The Germans challenged the British much more directly over the Cameroons. The Cameroons, lying between the Oil Rivers and Gabon, were regarded as a desirable region because they were healthier than most of the neighbouring territories. Britain had old established commercial interests there and the local chiefs had several times asked for British protection in the 1870s. The British government, which was still trying to avoid any extension of its African responsibilities, had refused. Two German firms were established in the Cameroons in 1880 but the British government was unalarmed. Nevertheless when the British government decided, in May 1884, to order Consul Hewett to strengthen its position on the Niger by concluding treaties with the African chiefs, it was decided to adopt the same policy in the Cameroons. It was still the French, not the Germans, they feared, and Hewett was instructed to go first to the Niger because the greater danger was apprehended there. So little did the British government fear the Germans that when the latter asked the British to assist a German agent, the well-known explorer, Gustav Nachtigal, to go to the Cameroons for scientific and commercial purposes, they readily agreed. Only in July 1884 did they learn that Nachtigal had used his visit to the Cameroons to sign treaties with the local chiefs, establishing a German protectorate (**31**, **47**, **99**, **107**). There was an understandable outcry from the British commercial interests involved. It is interesting, however, that at first they felt able only to ask that the British government would ensure that their trade was not discriminated against. Only later do they ask for direct British intervention and annexations to protect their trade [**docs 12d, 13**].

In the middle of 1884 annexation and the assumption of direct political, responsibilities were quite foreign to the British tradition in tropical Africa. Britons had previously done very well under a system of 'informal influence' (**96**). The situation was quite altered by the sudden new activity of France and Germany and the new 'rules of the game' laid down by the Berlin Conference [**docs 13, 14**].

Despite the link with the Egyptian imbroglio suggested by Professors Robinson and Gallagher (96) and accepted in a restricted form by other writers, including Professors Stengers (149) and Hargreaves (47), the 'Scramble' proper seems to have begun in West Africa. Various explanations have been offered – the entry of a maverick individual, Leopold II, into the game, or Bismarck's sudden decision to use Africa as a pawn in his European diplomacy. That there was an important diplomatic dimension to the struggle is undeniable. It is also true, as Robinson and Gallaher insist, that in the last resort the decisions were government decisions taken by cabinets and foreign offices. But what moved a reluctant British government to act was the recognition that British trade was in danger and that, in the last resort, the government had a duty to protect that trade, even if it meant an unpleasant extension of political responsibility. At home pressure was exerted on the government, not by bankers or financiers, but by traders.

The traders who organised themselves to protect their interests are an identifiable group. The same names reappear time and time again on petitions and deputations, supported by M.P.s who sat for the great manufacturing areas. Manchester was the centre of the movement. Manchester was the capital of the great cotton industry, Britain's leading export industry of the nineteenth century, which was comparatively much more important than, say, the car industry is today; 80 per cent of Britain's cotton manufactures were exported and she held more than 80 per cent of the world trade in cotton goods (97). African markets, although they accounted for only a small part of the whole (6 per cent in the 1880s), were important to the Manchester men (94). West African markets appeared to be growing rapidly. The Board of Trade prepared some figures for the Foreign Office in November 1884 which showed that British exports to British possessions in West Africa had increased from £340,366 in 1860 to £855,486 in 1883. Cotton manufactures accounted for £558,770 worth of this; 'Apparel and haberdashery' for £39,605. The other important items were hardware and cutlery – £23,400; metals, including iron, £20,550; arms, £10,462 and ammunition £9,438. These last figures help to explain why Manchester could usually rely on Sheffield and Birmingham to second its campaigns. Despite some internecine quarrels they could also usually command the support of the great ports, Liverpool, Glasgow and Bristol, with their ancient connections with the African trade [doc. 12].

British participation in the Scramble in West Africa was largely defensive, to protect existing interests against new competition. But both the new challenge from the continental powers and the strength of the British response may have had their roots in more general economic factors. Whereas during the greater part of the nineteenth century there had only been one highly industrialised power, Britain, which had supplied a large part of the world with its manufacturing requirements, there were now a number of competing industrial powers. The United States was getting into its stride again after the Civil War. Germany, united in 1871, and helped by the huge indemnity exacted from the defeated French, was industrialising at a rate that left Britain standing still. Even the France of the Third Republic, although slower off the mark than Germany, was modernising quickly. As a natural result of competitive conditions, nations were once again turning to protective tariff policies. Only Britain had committed herself completely to a free trade policy in the middle of the century. For many Britons free trade had indeed become almost a religious doctrine, a necessary precondition of peace, prosperity and international cooperation. In these circumstances Britain could hardly abandon it as an obsolete economic theory, but other nations had no such inhibitions. The United States never really relaxed the high tariffs they had put on during the abnormal circumstances of the Civil War. Germany reintroduced a protectionist tariff in 1879 — partly, it is true, for domestic and revenue reasons. France, which had never been a whole-hearted convert to free trade, reverted to traditional protectionist duties in 1882 (**19, 103**). British traders protested time and time again that their real objection to foreign protectorates was that they meant damage to British trade arising from discriminatory duties [**doc. 12**].

A shrill note was added to the complaints of the traders, German and French, as well as British, by the background fact of the 'Great Depression'. This depression, about which economic historians still argue vigorously (**102**), was marked by low prices, low profits, low interest rates, over production of certain commodities and, irregularly, high unemployment. It affected most of western Europe. It began with a financial crisis in 1873 and lasted, with varying degrees of intensity, until 1896. Germany and Britain were badly affected in the 1870s. In France the main effect was not felt until the 1880s. In Germany the French indemnity had proved a two-edged weapon. After an initial boom hundreds of companies had gone bankrupt in 1873. By 1879 both British and German economists were seriously alarmed. The depression had already lasted longer than was normal and there seemed no way out of it. Some men in both countries began to think in terms of colonial solutions. A few bold men in Britain began to ask for 'Fair Trade', a euphemism for the taboo word 'Protection' (**113**). They also began to ask for a parliamentary enquiry. This was eventually set up in 1885 and issued a massive report at the end of 1886. It was one of the most thorough enquiries ever conducted into the state of British industry in the nineteenth century. The Commission called for evidence, not only from government experts but also from chambers of commerce and employers' and working men's associations. The evidence revealed deep and widespread anxieties. There was a great division of opinion as to how the crisis should be met but many spoke of the need for new markets and a few spoke specifically of the existing colonies and of the new possibilities of Africa [doc. 16].

It would be wrong to see a massive or articulate public demand for imperial expansion in the mid-1880s, but the climate of opinion had undoubtedly changed. Britain's industrial position was now challenged and with it the prosperity of all classes of her population, Lancashire cotton workers as much as city businessmen, and this was widely realised. There was a distinct disposition to hang on to everything Britain had and not to shrink from new acquisitions, if this kept them out of the hands of a rival. The government was affected by this as well as the public. There was little logic about Britain's large acquisitions of territory in tropical Africa in the mid-1880s. They were essentially an anxious, even panicky, reaction to new challenges in an already worrying situation.

5 East Africa

Britain gained large areas in West Africa, including the whole of the modern Nigeria, as a direct result of the Scramble. She also acquired vast tracts of East Africa. The simplest and most likely explanation of the West African acquisitions is defence of trade. But Britain had nothing like such an old and well-established trading connection with East Africa as with West. Can the same explanation hold good there? Some authorities have suggested that it cannot, that, although trade may have been the dominant motive in West Africa, in the East strategy was more important. This is powerfully argued by Professors Robinson and Gallagher who go further and contend: 'The concentration on east Africa shows the preoccupation with supreme strategic interests. ... Trade prospects had always seemed better in western than in eastern regions. ... Yet ... the late Victorians ... preferred to make the empire safer in the poorer east Africa than to make it wealthier in the richer west' (96).

There is much that is attractive in this thesis. The East Coast had always had close links with India. The British Consulate at Zanzibar was under the jurisdiction of the Government of India until 1883 — although it should be noted that this was a recognition of the importance of British Indian subjects in the trade of Zanzibar (an importance that continued well into the period of the Scramble) as well as of the possible significance of East African ports lying on the Cape route to India [doc. 17d] (29, 86). Until 1869 the Cape route was the main sea route to India. Even after the opening of the Suez Canal many regarded it as the safer route in time of crisis [doc. 6d]. It was natural therefore that Britain should be reluctant to see a rival great power installed on the East Coast of Africa. The British reaction to the French acquisition of Madagascar in 1883-85 leads one to doubt, however, whether this motive was so central to British policy as is sometimes suggested. The French not only forcibly installed a protectorate on that island, which lay much more athwart the route to India than did the ports of East Africa, but also roughly handled British missionary and other interests in the process. The British government, however, embarrassed by other problems in Egypt, decided 'to put no difficulties in the way of the French' (43). The Admiralty, when asked in 1886 how much importance they attached to the harbour of Mombasa, replied that it would be of little use to them in war time. In the last resort, the safety of the Cape route to India depended upon Britain's maintenance of control of the high seas. If she lost that, additional bases would be no use to her; so long as she retained it they were on the whole unnecessary[1] [doc. 17d].

For many years Britain was content with the informal influence she exercised over the Sultan of Zanzibar. In 1873 it was strengthened by the appointment as Consul General of Sir John Kirk, who attained a degree of influence which has been compared to that which Stratford Canning once exercised at Constantinople. The British persuaded Sultan Barghash to sign a treaty suppressing the Slave Trade. They supported the Sultan diplomatically when the Khedive Ismail supplemented his expansionist policy in the Sudan by occupying certain East African ports over which the Sultan claimed jurisdiction. A British naval officer, Lloyd William Mathews, built up an efficient army for the Sultan. By 1877 the Sultan was prepared to consider placing himself under British protection (29, 53, 86). The British, however, were not alone at Zanzibar. German firms, first Herz and Sons, later Hansing and O'Swald, had been active there since the 1840s. It was only a matter of time before the Sultan learnt that it was possible to play the two powers off against one another (107).

In 1877-78, however, British influence was dominant. The explorations of the previous twenty years had begun to make men realise that the interior of East Africa might be valuable for its own sake. The populous African kingdom of Buganda on Lake Victoria seemed to offer considerable trading possibilities. The highlands, particularly the area round Mount Kilimanjaro, might even be suitable for extensive European settlement. Enthusiasts began to suggest that East Africa might be not only a new India but a new Australia [doc. 17c]. A group of Englishmen, led by the Scottish shipowner, Sir William Mackinnon, who in 1872 had organised the first regular mail service between Britain, India and Zanzibar, put forward an ambitious scheme in 1877, under which they would administer the whole vast area from the coast to Lake Victoria in the name of the Sultan. The failure of the scheme is one of the most extraordinary stories in the history of the Scramble for Africa, indeed in the history of British diplomacy. The Foreign Secretary, Lord Salisbury, while pretending to approve the project, sent out

---

[1] See the present author's article, 'Clement Hill's memoranda and the British interest in East Africa', *English Historical Review*, LXXXVII, July 1972.

an eccentric orientalist, G. P. Badger, ostensibly to help with legal forms but in reality with secret instructions to wreck the scheme. Badger so irritated and offended the Sultan that the latter refused to give his consent (86).

Salisbury had been determined that there should be no extension of British responsibilities in East Africa. His views were shared by William Gladstone, who a few years later was to lament that his cabinet colleagues could become so excited about the fate of the 'mountain with an unrememberable name [Kilimanjaro]' (43). But in East Africa, as in West, the situation had changed. There was now a new German challenge, and the pressure from British commercial interests for government protection for their interests had built up to a new level.

One of the strongest advocates of the establishment of an English colony in the region of Mount Kilimanjaro was H. H. Johnston (87). 'Here is a land', he wrote 'eminently suited for European colonisation, situated midway between the Equatorial lakes and the coast. Within a few years it must be either English, French or German'. If a road could be made into the interior, 'trade will flow entirely into English hands; the ivory, wax, iron, hides of the interior will come to our markets'. He was fortunate in obtaining the wholehearted support of the British Consul at Zanzibar, Frederick Holmwood. Holmwood communicated directly with the Manchester merchants, led by James Hutton. Hutton in turn enlisted the support of Lord Aberdare and others who were contemporaneously supporting him on West Africa. These arguments impressed a number of individuals both in the Foreign Office and in the Cabinet, but Gladstone set his face firmly against a forward policy in East Africa and, for a time, his views prevailed [docs. 17a-17d].

It was German activity which changed the situation. In 1884 the German explorer, Karl Peters, went to East Africa. He had been warned before he set out that he had no official status and could not look to his government for support. Despite this, he concluded a number of treaties with chiefs who swore that they were independent of the Sultan of Zanzibar in the general area of what later became Tanganyika. Peters returned to Berlin in February 1885, and on 3 March, the day after the Berlin West Africa Conference dispersed, the German government publicly proclaimed that it would take the territories secured by Peters under its protection.

The British merchants and their supporters redoubled their pressure on the Foreign Office, and suggested taking up again the Mackinnon scheme of 1877. The Liberal Government fell from office in June 1885, but, as in the Niger region, it is interesting that there is no significant difference in the way in which the Conservatives and the Liberals proposed to deal with the situation. Britain, Germany and France agreed to the setting up, in November 1885, of a Boundary Commission to determine the legal limits of the Sultan's domain. As for the inland areas which would probably be judged to lie beyond the Sultan's territories, both Conservative and Liberals felt that a modified version of the Mackinnon scheme would now be the best solution if an agreement could be reached with Germany. An agreement was finally reached in October 1886 which left the coast under the jurisdiction of the Sultan but allocated what became Kenya and Uganda to Britain and Tanganyika to Germany. So far as the administration of the British sphere was concerned the British government resorted to the same device as on the Niger, a chartered company. In 1888 the Imperial British East Africa Company, headed by Sir William Mackinnon, was chartered. James Hutton was on its board of directors (**29, 86**).

On the east coast of Africa there were undoubtedly strategic considerations which did not apply anywhere on the west coast, but so far as the division of the hinterland in 1886 was concerned exactly the same factors seem to have operated as operated on the Niger. British merchants, centred on, although not confined to, Manchester, with a number of supporters in public life, had fought a fierce battle to prevent a region which might one day be important to British commerce passing under the control of another great power [**docs. 17a-17c**]. No one claimed that the commercial benefits would be immediate. They were, as Rosebery was to say, in mining language, 'pegging out claims' (**56**). A great inflow of capital was necessary before any return could be seen, in particular a railway from Mombasa to Lake Victoria, the famous 'Uganda Railway', was essential (**86**). Moreover, it slowly became clear that the economic development of East Africa was to be different from that of West Africa. In West Africa the economy was essentially that of peasant proprietors. In the East the development of cash crops meant a plantation economy to grow cotton and coffee. Neither the capital nor the settlers were quickly forthcoming (**11**). Even in 1902 there were less than a dozen European families farming in Kenya. The lack of capital, above all for railway development, was crippling to the Imperial British East Africa Company. By the early 1890s it was virtually bankrupt. The history of the British East Africa Company, and of the German chartered companies which suffered similar financial difficulties, seems almost sufficient in itself to demolish the theory that it was 'surplus capital' seeking foreign outlets which caused the annexations of the late nineteenth century. Far from capital fighting to get out, it was almost impossible to persuade it to go.

Naturally disillusionment set in. Vast tracts of Africa had been acquired in a moment of panic in the mid-1880s. Salisbury himself commented on the extraordinary nature of the phenomenon. When he left the Foreign Office in 1880, he said, no one thought of Africa, when he returned in 1885 the whole of Europe was quarrelling about it (26). Once the moment of panic and 'grab' had passed some men began to return to their earlier views that colonies were expensive and vulnerable and that caution should be exercised in acquiring them. Bismarck himself commented wryly, 'I am not a colonial man.' New factors had however, now come into play. As the British had found over the Gambia it was surprisingly difficult to relinquish territory (see above p. 49). Some interest group was bound to be offended and there was an irrational, but nonetheless powerful reluctance to abandon a country over which one's flag had once flown. Central Africa was no longer *terra incognita*. European ambitions and interests were established there. New strategic considerations now developed, connected with Africa itself. Colonies had been established. They must be protected and their boundaries and communication routes made as rational as possible. The year 1890 saw a whole series of agreements between Britain and other European powers. These were essentially 'tidying up' agreements, arising from the hasty arrangements of 1884-86. They have, however, a different quality about them from the earlier negotiations. In Britain this is probably partly only a reflection of the different 'styles' of Salisbury and Granville. Granville was pushed into almost all the decisions he made in 1884-85 by unexpected circumstances. Salisbury, possibly in 1886, certainly by 1889-90, was beginning to play something like the 'Great Game' of Central Asia, transferred to an African context and to enjoy it. This is very far from saying that Salisbury had become converted to a forward imperialist policy in Africa. Probably he was never that (26, 96). But he had had time to assess the situation, to determine what objectives were worth pursuing and even to make Africa play a part in his European diplomacy.

The most important of the agreements Britain made in 1890 was with Germany. Bismarck may have been feeling his way towards a more general understanding with Britain but he fell from power before the agreement was finally reached. By it Germany recognised a British protectorate over the dominions of the Sultan of Zanzibar. In return the Germans got some small concessions in West Africa, the famous Caprivi Strip – a corridor of land connecting German South West Africa with the Zambesi – and the island of Heligoland in the North Sea which had been in British hands since the Napoleonic Wars (134,

135, 147). France also recognised the British protectorate over Zanzibar in return for a British recognition of the French position in Madagascar. Portugal acknowledged the British position in Mashonaland and Nyasaland (see below, p. 79) in return for the acceptance of other boundary claims on behalf of Portuguese East Africa (26, 62, 65).

A little ironically, however, the final decision about a British retention of Uganda had to be made by a Liberal Government, once again headed by William Gladstone. By this time the question had been complicated by religious strife and new strategic considerations. Until the 1860s the Baganda had been pagans, but traders from Zanzibar brought the Islamic faith with them. The Kabaka (king), Mutesa, was interested and, from 1867, adopted at least some Moslem observances. Henry Morton Stanley, however, on his visit in 1875 drew attention to the rival claims of Christianity. Mutesa, perhaps for political reasons, again expressed interest. In 1877 representatives of the Anglican Church Missionary Society arrived. In 1879 the Roman Catholic White Fathers, sent by the 'Apostle of Africa', Cardinal Lavigerie, came. Soon there were three rival parties, Muslim, English Protestant and French Catholic. Mutesa died in 1884 and his successor Mwanga did not share his sympathy for Christian missionaries. In 1885-86 European attention was attracted to Uganda; first, by the murder on Mwanga's orders, of an Anglican bishop, James Hannington; and, secondly, by the massacre of thirty of Mwanga's pages, Catholic converts who refused to recant. By the late 1880s Uganda was in a state of civil war (54, 86).

In 1890 the British East Africa Company sent a man later to be famous as Governor of Nigeria, Captain Lugard, to try to establish the Company's authority in Buganda. A subsequent British Chancellor of the Exchequer, Sir William Harcourt, later blamed the Company for rushing into Uganda, instead of building up their sphere slowly from the coast (38). The Company in turn protested that they had no wish to go to Uganda so soon, but had been pushed into it by the government who wished to make sure that the area would not slip into German hands, despite the preliminary division of 1886. They had reason to worry. Karl Peters himself had been active in the region, signing treaties with chiefs early in 1890. But the Anglo-German agreement concluded later that year meant that the German government never accepted the treaties (86, 90).

The British East Africa Company, however, had reached its financial limit. In December 1890 Mackinnon asked the government to guarantee the interest on the capital they wished to raise to build the railway from Mombasa to Lake Victoria (86). Salisbury himself was well disposed, but the strength of parliamentary opposition was such that the proposal was dropped in July 1891 (**26**). When the Conservatives left office in August 1892 the future of Uganda was still unresolved although the East Africa Company was insisting that, unless they received a substantial subvention, total evacuation was inevitable. Evacuation would have been entirely acceptable to some members of the Liberal Cabinet, including Harcourt, John Morley and Gladstone himself [**doc. 18**]. They attached little importance to Uganda, they disliked Lugard's forward policy there; and they lived in mortal dread of a new 'Gordon incident' (**38, 80**). Against them, however, were ranged very powerful missionary interests, which had already contributed substantial funds to keep a British presence in Uganda, and which feared a new massacre of Christian converts if Britain withdrew. The East Africa Company, despite its precarious financial position, managed to rally significant support from Chambers of Commerce and trading organisations. But the decisive fact was undoubtedly that the new Foreign Secretary, Lord Rosebery, committed himself completely to a retentionist policy. It may well be, as R. R. James suggests, that there was a considerable element of domestic political manoeuvring in this. Rosebery wished to worst Harcourt and demonstrate that he was the only possible successor to the aged Gladstone (**56**). But it is also true that Rosebery was a man of the younger generation, an imperialist at least in the sense of believing that colonies were valuable and should be defended, a world apart from Gladstone or his own predecessor, Granville. Rosebery prevailed. Uganda was retained and a formal protectorate proclaimed there in 1894.

Uganda now had a strategic importance that it had never had in the past. Until 1887 British governments, both Liberal and Conservative, had been sincere in their avowed intention to end the occupation of Egypt as soon as possible. The muddled events of 1882 had left them in Egypt without any proper status in international law. It had strained their relations with France. The new Egyptian financial crisis of 1885, resulting partly from events in the Sudan, had meant a new international loan and the involvement of still more powers, Russia and Italy among them, in the control of the Egyptian finances. Britain was in effect administering Egypt without controlling the purse strings. Foreign powers, and Liberals at home, could and did taunt British governments with their failure to carry out their earlier evacuation promises, and foreign powers could always apply diplomatic pressure in Egypt. It became, as a later Foreign Secretary, Sir Edward Grey, said, a noose round Britain's neck that other powers could tighten at will (**42**). In these circumstances Sir Henry Drummond Wolff's mission to Constantinople in 1885 to try to secure a British withdrawal upon conditions that would still protect British interests, was entirely sincere. A convention was in fact signed with the Turks in May 1887 providing for British evacuation within three years but since it also allowed for re-entry in some circumstances, the Sultan eventually decided not to ratify it. From 1887 onwards Salisbury's policy (and Rosebery's) was determined by the fact that Britain was in Egypt for the foreseeable future and that that position must be protected. Potentially hostile powers must be kept away from the sources and upper reaches of the Nile. The exact effect of this on British diplomacy has been much debated but the general influence is clear (41, 96, 101, 134, 135, 147).

Britain was in Egypt because she could not find a safe way of getting out, but she was also beginning to adopt a quite different attitude towards her position there. The administration of Egypt had been undertaken in the autumn of 1882 because there was no alternative. By the late 1880s it was becoming the showpiece of beneficient British imperialism in action. The Egyptian economy was fundamentally sound. Well administered and with a government much better placed than the Khedive's had been to resist international pressures, the country was now very prosperous. In 1883 Cromer had been strongly in favour of early evacuation [doc. 8b]. By 1886 he had changed his mind. Joseph Chamberlain, who had had so many misgivings about the occupation [doc. 8a], visited Egypt and, in the words of his official biographer (39), 'became whole as an imperialist'. In 1892 one of Cromer's assistants, Alfred Milner, published his *England in Egypt*, hymning the British achievements there (77). The British began to acquire a comfortable conviction that they were a natural 'governing race', with a mission to bring good government and liberal ideas to the whole world [doc. 26].

Egypt also lay at one end of the famous Cape to Cairo railway project which first began to receive serious attention in 1889. It is probably true that neither Salisbury nor his principal Foreign Office advisers, such as Lister's successor, Sir Percy Anderson, ever took it altogether seriously (138). In any case the final recognition of the German sphere in Tanganyika in 1890 seemed to cut across any hope of an all-red route from north to south but the possibility of a line through Katanga with the consent of Leopold of the Belgians remained. When Kitchener began to lay a railway into the Sudan in 1896 in the course of the reconquest of that region (see below p. 84) he chose the same gauge as that in use at the Cape. By the 1890s planning was on a continental scale. Men like Salisbury were playing diplomatic chess with the whole of Africa (41).

6 South Africa

In southern Africa the one man who could undoubtedly 'think big' was Cecil John Rhodes [doc. 19]. Rhodes had arrived in South Africa in 1870, a thin, tubercular young man, sent to regain his health on his brother's cotton farm in Natal. He spent most of the next few years not in Natal, but on the new diamond diggings at Kimberley. The first diamond had been found there in 1867. For some time the children of a Boer farmer had played with the 'pretty marble' before its value was discovered. Kimberley, perhaps more than anywhere else, symbolised the El Dorado element in the new Africa. Griqualand West, where the diamond diggings were, quickly attracted an overflowing population, old prospectors from America and Australia, petty crooks from the East End of London, the whole choir, according to one report, of the cathedral of Grahamstown (55). It was a tough society but Rhodes quickly made his mark. His first big *coup* was to corner the market in pumping equipment when the workings were threatened with disastrous flooding. But Rhodes was a great deal more than a smart operator. Otherwise he would have finished up merely as a rich man like some of his rivals on the diamond fields, Alfred Beit or Barney Barnato. Rhodes was always a dreamer too. He spent long nights on the veldt philosophising to anyone who would listen, and he commuted from Kimberley to Oxford intermittently between 1873 and 1881 to obtain a degree. Rhodes retained an almost mystic faith in the powers of education, which was later to bear fruit in his endowment of 'Rhodes scholarships' to take young men from the Empire, the United States and Germany to Oxford (64, 110).

Rhodes's dream was of the British empire. He became convinced of the peculiar destiny of the Anglo-Saxon peoples to govern the world beneficently. He regarded the American War of Independence as the greatest tragedy that had occurred in modern times and hoped that one day the United States would reunite with the other English-speaking countries in a new federal empire. Rhodes had the odd habit of expressing his political views in a series of 'Last Wills and Testaments' which he compiled throughout his life. One of the strangest was that of 1877, in which he envisaged the incorporation into the empire of the whole of

Africa, much of the Middle East, including the Holy Land, the whole of South America, the islands of the Pacific, Malaya and the seaboard of China and Japan. He considered founding a secret society, a 'secular order of Jesuits', to further the interests of the empire [doc. 19b]. The dreams sounded too extravagant to be taken seriously but Rhodes was above all a 'doer' — the one type of man he thoroughly despised was what he called a 'loafer'. By his early thirties he was a multi-millionaire but he had little interest in money for its own sake. He generally dressed like a tramp and kept no careful account of his wealth. He wanted money for the power it brought [doc. 19a]. In 1880 he plunged into South African politics, becoming M.P. for a Griqualand constituency, Barkly West.

South African politics were already in a tangled state. The story goes back to the British acquisition of the Cape during the Napoleonic Wars. The existing settlers, the Boers, bitterly resented the 'anglicising' policy of the British and, more especially, their 'native policy'. By the famous Fiftieth Ordnance of 1828 the British greatly improved the civil rights of the Hottentots, and in 1833 they abolished slavery throughout the empire with what the Boers regarded as totally inadequate compensation. The Boers had always been used to 'trekking' in search of new land and now a mass movement, the Great Trek, began. They went first to Natal but the British disliked the idea of a colony on the South African coast not under their control, which might fall under the influence of another great power. In 1845 they annexed Natal. The Boers moved on, first to what became the Orange Free State and later to what became the Transvaal. The British, in the middle of the century, were interested only in the Cape as a staging post to India. The fewer responsibilities they had in the interior the better they liked it. By the Sand River Convention of 1852 and the Bloemfontein Convention of 1854 respectively they recognised the independence of the Transvaal and the Orange Free State. But the tension between the two peoples continued. Many Boers still lived in Cape Colony and some in Natal. The two peoples never saw eye to eye about 'native policy'. The British felt that the Boers by their continual clashes with the Bantu were stirring up trouble for the whole of southern Africa — although without fundamentally understanding the very complex population movements of the interior. (See Chapter 1 above.) Not only the Boers but some British South Africans felt that the government in London had very little appreciation of the peculiar difficulties that they faced and resentment at what was generally called the 'imperial factor', that is, intervention in South African affairs from London, grew accordingly (59, 60, 108).

The situation grew more acute in the 1870s. The Boer republic resented the British annexation of Griqualand West after the diamond discoveries. The legal claims of Cape Colony and the Transvaal to the area are not easy to disentangle but confidence was not inspired by the fact that the matter was referred to the arbitration of the British Governor of Natal, Robert Keate. Lord Carnarvon, Colonial Secretary in Disraeli's government of 1874, impressed by the success of Canadian federation in 1867, hoped that all the problems of South Africa might be solved by a federation of the four states, Cape Colony, Natal, the Orange Free State and the Transvaal. Carnarvon's plans broke down, however, on one vital point. The Canadians had actively desired federation; the South Africans did not. Nevertheless the Transvaalers could no longer go on alone. Their Treasury was almost empty and they were faced with a great new military threat from the resurgent Zulu power under Cetewayo. In these circumstances Sir Theophilus Shepstone, the Secretary for Native Affairs in Natal, was able to rush the Transvaalers into accepting annexation to the British Crown. The new British Governor of Cape Colony, Sir Bartle Frere, who had come to South Africa from India with a high reputation for both efficiency and enlightenment, had now to decide how to deal with the Zulus. London, faced with a probable war in Afghanistan, instructed him to damp down the South African situation. Frere, however, had already issued an ultimatum to the Zulus demanding the demobilisation of their large standing army. The Zulus refused to comply and inflicted a serious defeat on a British force which they caught unprepared at Isandhlwana. A war lasting several months followed which ended with the defeat of the Zulus and the surrender of Cetewayo (81).

So long as they were threatened by the Zulus the Boers of the Transvaal remained passive but, after Cetewayo's final defeat, they protested that the annexation of 1877 had been forced upon them and demanded the return of their independence. Gladstone and the Liberal party in England accepted the validity of their arguments but when Gladstone came into office in 1880 Boer independence was not immediately restored. The Liberals, like Carnarvon, had some hope that a South African federation might come out of the troubles. The Boers, however, declined to wait. They defeated a British force at Majuba Hill in 1881. Some men in Britain counselled the government to 'avenge Majuba' before making concessions, but Gladstone refused. Instead two conventions were signed with the Boers, that of Pretoria of 1881 and that of London of 1884. There was unfortunately some ambiguity about these Conventions. They clearly restored internal autonomy to the Transvaal, but the 1881 Convention had a preamble (not repeated in

1884) asserting British suzerainty. The Transvaal was precluded from certain acts which would have been economically damaging to the other South African states. The Transvaal insisted that the Conventions had restored them, for all practical purposes, to the status of an independent state. The British government, however, held — and this view was to be very strongly stated by a later Colonial Secretary, Joseph Chamberlain (39) — that it was a limited and conditional independence that left the British government free, not only to control the Transvaal's external relations with other powers, but in some circumstances to intervene in her internal affairs.

The abortive British annexation of the Transvaal was the most spectacular extension of British responsibilities in South Africa in this period but there had been others. In 1868 they had annexed Basutoland (the modern Lesotho). This too had been the result of friction between Africans and Boers. The Basuto people were basically the scattered elements of a number of tribes which had survived the onslaughts of Chaka. They had found a leader of outstanding ability in Moshesh. Their numbers began to expand and in the 1850s they and the advancing Boers began to compete for fertile land. In despair Moshesh appealed for British protection and, reluctantly, the British agreed (81, 108).

In the 1880s all eyes began to focus on the vast area of Bechuanaland. Bechuanaland was on the whole an infertile territory but through it passed what was then called the 'Missionaries' Road', although it was an important route long before the Christian missionaries came. Cecil Rhodes himself called it South Africa's 'Suez Canal'. To the west were Damaraland and Namaqualand which were to become (see pp. 58-59 above) German South West Africa. To the east were the Boer Republics, themselves in an expansionist mood. If Cape Colony did not act quickly she must resign herself to seeing her route to the north occupied by others. To some this might seem of no great moment but to Cecil Rhodes and his supporters it was vital. Rhodes was already dreaming of an expansion of British South Africa, perhaps as far north as the Great Lakes. Even in the more limited context of the existing South African states it was fundamental to the future balance of power. One day there almost certainly would be some kind of federation. Would it be dominated by the Boers or by the British? It seemed likely that whichever side gained a significant accretion of power now would finally dominate the southern part of the continent. In 1885, startled by German actions in South West Africa, the British government finally moved. Bechuanaland south of the Molopo River became a Crown Colony, north of the river a British protectorate (110, 64).

Despite the British acquisition of Bechuanaland in the following year, 1886, the balance of power in South Africa suddenly began to tilt in favour of the Boers. In that year the great gold discoveries were made on the Witwatersrand. The discoveries were in one sense very unwelcome to the traditionalist Boers, led by the old Voortrekker, Paul Kruger. They wanted to live their traditional pastoral life, uninterrupted by a gold rush and the influx of thousands of, in their eyes, undesirable foreigners into their state. On the other hand, if political power followed economic power, the Transvaal was well placed to become the dominant state.

Meanwhile Cecil Rhodes was preparing his next move. He was among the first to buy a substantial stake in the Witwatersrand. This gave him a financial edge over some of his old rivals on the diamond fields. In 1888 he persuaded a rather reluctant Nathaniel Rothschild to back him in a financial operation which forced his greatest rival, Barney Barnato (Rufus Isaacs, the East End Jew who had gone to South Africa in 1873 with forty boxes of dubious cigars belonging to his brother-in-law as his sole asset, 55) to amalgamate his interests with those of Rhodes in the De Beers Consolidated Mines Company, which still virtually controls the world diamond market. The trust deed of the new company was an extraordinary one. It did not confine its activities to diamond mining but deliberately opened the way for Rhodes to 'go north', by allowing its capital to be used to administer and develop any area.

Rhodes had his eyes firmly fixed on the region north of the Transvaal, Mashonaland and Matabeleland. The story of how he secured what was to become Southern Rhodesia (and today simply Rhodesia) is not an edifying one, although one should perhaps bear in mind, as Dr Hanna suggests (46), that the regime that the British replaced was itself a brutal tyranny based on conquest. The area had originally been occupied by the Mashona, a peaceful pastoral people, but, some forty years before the British became seriously interested in the area, the Matabele, an offshoot of the Zulus, under Mzilikazi, had turned north and conquered them (81). Mzilikazi was in time succeeded by his son Lobengula. The nature of Matabele rule was such that, in trying to determine the limit of Lobengula's dominions, the only question that could meaningfully be asked seemed to be 'Has he raided there?' [doc. 21].

Lobengula was, according to all contemporary accounts, an impressive figure; a shrewd man who did all that in him lay to prevent his country being taken by the Europeans, whether it was restraining his own young men from a premature challenge or trying to beat the Europeans at their own diplomatic game (75). That he lost is a reflection of the fact that the odds were too heavily stacked against him. By the 1880s Lobengula was a sorely tried man. It was generally believed that Mashonaland was very rich in gold. Geologically, this seemed to make sense. The gold deposits of the Witwatersrand were now known, the mineral wealth of Katanga suspected. It seemed likely that a crescent of wealth stretched through the future Rhodesia. Moreover, men like the German, Karl Peters, had argued very persuasively that Mashonaland was probably the site of the legendary gold mines of King Solomon (91). (Rider Haggard incorporated the idea in a famous novel, *King Solomon's Mines*.) If the Phoenicians had mined gold there that would explain the great ruins of Zimbabwe which Victorians could not believe that Africans had built. Lobengula was besieged by concession hunters of all nationalities, British, Portuguese, German and Boer. Lobengula rightly discerned that the Boers and the Portuguese were interested in his land as well as in mineral rights. He wrongly concluded that the British were probably only concerned with the minerals [doc. 20].

Rhodes did hope to find gold in Mashonaland. The experience of the British East Africa Company had shown that only reasonable profits quickly would keep investors interested. In Rhodes's own famous phrase, the ideal combination was 'philanthropy plus 5 per cent'. For Rhodes, however, financial profit was now a secondary consideration – fortunately perhaps for him, since he made no profit out of Rhodesia. He wanted to attract British settlers into the region for a number of reasons; the general principle of expanding the British empire, to keep the balance of South Africa British, to keep alive the dream of an all-red route from the Cape to Cairo which had many attractions for Rhodes. He was influenced too by the general arguments current about the need for empire building. He wrote to W. T. Stead in 1891 that markets were the key question since English home consumption could only support six million workers (95). Then there is the famous passage, quoted by Lenin, in which Rhodes recounted how he attended a meeting of the unemployed in the East End in 1895 and 'listened to the wild speeches, which were just a cry for "bread", "bread", "bread",' and became convinced that the only alternative to civil war was that 'we colonial statesmen must acquire new lands to settle the surplus population, to provide new markets for the goods produced in the factories and mines' (119). However wild some of his dreams, the empire remained for Rhodes essentially 'a bread and butter question'.

In 1887 two Boers, the Grobler brothers, obtained a treaty from Lobengula which purported to give them very considerable rights, including rights of passage through his territory and the right to call on him for military assistance. The treaty was suspect since it was not in a language Lobengula could understand and there were no independent witnesses to testify that it had been properly translated to him. Lobengula subsequently repudiated it. The incident of the Grobler treaty moved the British authorities to persuade Lobengula to sign a treaty, witnessed by a missionary he trusted, John Moffat, agreeing not to enter into correspondence or treaties with foreign powers, or sell, alienate or cede any part of his country without the previous agreement of the British High Commissioner in South Africa (**75**).

Lobengula now came to the plausible, but as it proved disastrous, conclusion that he could get rid of a lot of the quarrelling concession seekers by giving monopoly rights to one group. He signed an agreement, the famous Rudd Concession [**doc. 20**] with C. D. Rudd, the emissary of Cecil Rhodes, by which, in return for money and weapons, he granted exclusive mineral rights to Rudd and his associates with certain vague clauses which conferred ill-defined additional rights to allow them to defend and administer their mining concession.

Rhodes was now ready to take his next step of seeking a Chartered Company to administer the whole region. Many obstacles, however, still remained. Other interested parties, notably the Bechuanaland Exploration Company, had to be bought out or induced to amalgamate their interests with his. Rhodes himself was by no means *persona grata* in England. He was still very active in Cape politics – he became Prime Minister of the Cape in 1890 – and his position was dependent on the close association he maintained with Boer politicians there. Moreover, he had always been an outspoken opponent of the 'imperial factor', if it seemed to encroach in any way upon the autonomy of Cape politics. In the circumstances it is not surprising that he was regarded in London, however mistakenly, as a Boer supporter and therefore suspect from an imperial point of view. He had powerful enemies in London. He had quarrelled with missionary interests over Bechuanaland. The Colonial Secretary, Lord Knutsford, originally supported the claims of the rival Bechuanaland Exploration Society. The London Chamber of Commerce opposed him. So did the Parliamentary South African committee which included not only Joseph Chamberlain, who deeply distrusted him, but also a number of men later closely associated with Rhodes such as the Duke of Fife and Albert, later Earl, Grey (**64**).

It was the greatest political feat of Rhodes's life that he overcame all this in the summer of 1889 and emerged, in October, with his Charter. The whole story has never transpired but the general reasons why Salisbury's government finally accepted Rhodes's schemes are clear enough. They were convinced that it was necessary to establish a British presence in Mashonaland and Matabeleland to forestall the Germans,

Portuguese and Boers. The alternative to a chartered company was direct British administration with all its attendant expenses. The Treasury was not in a generous mood and the government was already experiencing the difficulties of running a colony on a shoestring in Bechuanaland. The change in the government attitude can be traced in Knutsford's communications with Lobengula. In March 1889, in a famous letter, he warned him to be cautious about giving away land or mining rights, reminding him that a prudent king might give a friendly stranger one ox, but not his whole herd of cattle. In November he advised him that, as he could not hope to exclude white men entirely, the safest course would be to agree with 'one approved body' (**26, 75**).

The Colonial Office later came to the conclusion that they had been deceived by Rhodes over the whole question of the Charter. They had not understood that the financial assets were retained by another company, the Central Search Association (later the United Concessions Company), which stood behind the Chartered Company. In strict law too the British government could only grant rights to their subjects as against other British subjects. They could not confer sovereign rights over Africans and African territories unless these were granted by treaty by the competent authorities. Rhodes performed a kind of sleight of hand by transforming vague rights connected with mining concessions into a territorial jurisdiction. All in all the Colonial Office concluded in 1892 they would be legally justified in cancelling the Charter. But it was politically impossible. The Chartered Company was the only body able and willing to keep the area in the British sphere [**doc. 21**].

If the Colonial Office had reason to complain that they had been deceived by Rhodes, Lobengula had more reason to protest. In his own eyes he repudiated the Rudd Concession by allowing the counsellor who advised him to sign it, Lotje, to be smelt out for witchcraft and by putting to death not only Lotje but his whole household. Lobengula was later to die, probably from smallpox, fleeing from Rhodes's forces, still trying to make clear to Rhodes that he no longer recognised their agreement by returning the money he had received under it.

All this did nothing to stop Rhodes's advance. He collected his 'Pioneers', a carefully selected body of men who marched into Mashonaland, at this stage avoiding Matabele territory proper, in the summer of 1890. In September 1890 they hoisted the Union Jack at an outpost, Fort Salisbury, and took possession of Mashonaland in the name of the Queen. The early pioneers suffered acutely from floods and near starvation conditions. Worse, the hopes of gold proved illusory. For a time Chartered shares boomed. Men and women almost fought for them. But soon they began to drift downwards. Randolph

Churchill visited the country and said openly there was no gold. The radical Labouchère began a great campaign against the Company in *Truth*. (75, 110).

Rhodes's stock was already falling at the time of the Jameson Raid in December 1895. An *uitlander* rising had been confidently expected in Johannesburg, where all new immigrants were denied the franchise and certain other rights by Kruger and the Boers. Joseph Chamberlain, the new British Colonial Secretary, undoubtedly knew of the projected rising – as did every well-informed man in London – and, since he took a very 'high' view of the rights which Britain retained under the 1881 and 1884 Conventions, he saw it as an excellent excuse to intervene on the break-down of law and order in the Transvaal. Rhodes, however, was the man primarily responsible for having a force standing by on the frontier under his old friend, Dr. Jameson, ready to intervene immediately and present the world with a *fait accompli*. Jameson alone was responsible for the mad act of going ahead with the invasion of the Transvaal when the rising itself had failed to materialise. Jameson was arrested by the Boers and handed over to the British authorities. Rhodes was compelled to resign as Prime Minister of the Cape. The repercussions went deep into British politics. There were many who never trusted Chamberlain again (39, 89, 92, 110, 132).

Rhodes feared most of all for his Charter and the new 'Rhodesia'. The Pioneers had penetrated, at the cost of war, into Matabeleland proper in 1893, but, with the withdrawal of security forces at the time of the Jameson Raid, first the Matabele and then, to everyone's astonishment, the Mashona, rose. The risings were put down with difficulty and Rhodes who, whatever his other failings, did not lack personal courage, met the African leaders in the Matoppo Hills to arrange a settlement. Mashonaland and Matabeleland were saved for the empire.

There was always an international dimension to the British position in southern Africa. In 1890 and 1891 respectively Salisbury had concluded agreements with Germany and Portugal delimiting their spheres in southern Africa (26). This enabled Britain in 1891 to include Barotseland, the modern Zambia, in the field of operations of the Chartered Company, to be known a few years later as Northern Rhodesia. The same year, 1891, they proclaimed a protectorate over Nyasaland where Scottish missions had for some time been active – so active indeed that boys from the Nyasaland mission schools were in demand for clerical positions all over southern Africa.

At the time of the Jameson Raid the Kaiser, William II, caused a sensation by sending a telegram to President Kruger, congratulating him on defending his independence without calling on the assistance of friendly powers. The British government tried to pass this off as a royal whim – in fact it had been sanctioned by William's political advisers – but it focused attention again on an old threat to Britain's position in South Africa. The British had always been concerned about German sympathy for the Boer Republics (**40**). They now concentrated particularly on trying to prevent the Boers getting an outlet to the sea through the Portuguese port of Lourenço Marques on Delagoa Bay. Despite the British opposition a railway from the Transvaal to Delagoa Bay was completed in 1894. The Boers were also buying in large stores of Krupps guns from Germany. By the time Alfred Milner went to South Africa as High Commissioner in 1899 both sides were ripe for a showdown. The outcome was the Boer War which dragged on from October 1899 until the Peace of Vereeniging in May 1902 (**45, 63**). The war, particularly the early ill-success of the British forces, came as a great shock to British opinion; the Liberal party split open. Some, including Lloyd George, sympathised with the Boer Republics, which they saw as small independent nations, 'bullied' by the might of the British empire. But the impact was more fundamental than that. Just as the death of Gordon had made men begin to question the whole Egyptian policy, so the Boer War made men begin to question the whole policy of the 'new imperialism' (see Part Three). Rhodes himself died, a few months before the end of the war, in March 1902, at the age of forty-nine, perhaps, as some of his obituaries said, a conquistador born out of time (**95**).

7 Fashoda and the Anglo-French Agreements of 1904

By 1898 the greater part of the continent of Africa was divided between the European powers. Liberia remained independent under the patronage of the United States. The Italians had failed spectacularly at the battle of Adowa in 1896 to make good their bid for Abyssinia. But these were the exceptions. The French had spread steadily over West and North West Africa. Morocco remained independent, but French influence was rapidly increasing there, displacing in some spheres old established British influence. French colonialists increasingly saw Morocco as the 'missing piece' of their empire, for which they might eventually be prepared to trade even Egypt [doc. 23] (78, 114).

The British had extended their colony of Sierra Leone to include the huge hinterland of the Protectorate in 1896, after a boundary agreement with France the previous year. The Gold Coast was the scene of new wars between the British and the Ashanti in 1895-96 and again in 1900-01. Ashantiland became a crown colony in 1901. The region north of Ashantiland, the so-called Northern Territories, occupied by a mixture of tribes, had been brought under British protection rather earlier in 1896-98 (33, 37, 61, 109).

In the Niger region, too, British territory had considerably expanded. The original British protectorate of 1885 extended only as far as the river Benue. The Royal Niger Company, however, had been active in penetrating into the Northern emirates, the well organised Muslim states such as Nupe and Ilorin, where good trade was expected. They met with many obstacles. The Liverpool men in the delta did not take kindly to the activities of this new Manchester-based group and did their best to discredit them at home until an accommodation was worked out in 1893 (36). The African middlemen, too, resented a new system of trading that seemed likely to cut out their profits. Some of them, of whom a selfmade man, Ja Ja of Opobo, was the most remarkable, put up a strong although ultimately unsuccessful resistance (57). The northern emirs were suspicious of the Company and examined all trading agreements very carefully. In the end the Company resorted to force of arms to overcome their resistance. But the most dangerous threat to the Company's position was to come from international complications, from the protests of France and Germany. The Company had interpreted the clauses of their Charter and of the Berlin Act which forbade the setting up of a monopoly and guaranteed free navigation on the Niger in their own way [**docs 14, 15**]. They bore the expenses of administering the area and, they argued, they did not intend to be out of pocket. Free navigation of the river was whittled down until it meant only freedom of transit, and any boat that touched at a wharf was regarded as coming under the Company's jurisdiction in respect of the revenue duties they were entitled to levy. Moreover, the Company evolved very neat book-keeping methods by which customs dues on their own goods were offset against 'administrative costs'. Since trading and government were so closely combined in the Company's activities almost any expense could be brought under the heading of 'administration'. Naturally there was soon a strong protest from foreign, especially German, traders, who felt themselves discriminated against. One result of the Liverpool and German opposition was the enquiry carried out for the British government by Major Macdonald in 1888. As Professor Flint demonstrates in his *Sir George Goldie and the Making of Nigeria* (**36**), Macdonald's enquiry was a landmark in British colonial policy in Africa. Macdonald tried to be fair to all parties including the Company but, in Flint's words, 'For him "Imperial interests" were the interests of the Africans'. It was the same principle that was to find expression forty years later in the Devonshire White Paper of 1923 which proclaimed without equivocation that 'Kenya is an African country'. Macdonald himself was careful to consult as many Africans as he could. Ideas of 'trusteeship', which had evolved in relation to India during, Edmund Burke's great attacks on Warren Hastings in the late eighteenth century, were real to many British officials and were translated from India to Africa (**36, 121**). In a world where the British government were the 'trustees' of the African masses, the rule of trading companies, primarily interested in their own profits, could have no place. The Royal Niger Company, unlike the Imperial British East Africa Company, was a financial success but its days were numbered. The Charter was surrendered in 1899 although the Company continued in being as an ordinary trading concern. By 1900 only Cecil Rhodes's South Africa Company remained. It was to last until 1923 and many commentators have traced the different development of Rhodesia in part to the lack of the official element which watched the interests of the weaker party, usually the native-born Africans, in the new British colonies (**123**). A subtle change had come over the whole British position in tropical Africa between the hasty 'grab' of 1884-86 and the end of the century. Initially, the government had had no thought but to establish spheres of influence to prevent the exclusion of British trade by foreign annexations. Now they found themselves ruling a colonial empire in Africa as they did in India. In West Africa the change was symbolised by the winding up of the Chartered Company in 1899 and the establishment in 1900 of the two huge protectorates of North and South Nigeria, joined together and including Lagos by 1914, to form the modern state of Nigeria, entirely the responsibility of the British government.

The Chartered Company came to an end in 1899 partly because views were changing as to Britain's proper relations with her African possessions, but also partly because the Company had over-extended itself in its conflicts with France. It was inevitable that, as the Company's dominion crept up the Niger, it would eventually clash with the expanding French West African empire. The confrontation came in the 1890s. Although tentative boundaries between the British and French spheres had been drawn up in 1890 many points were left unresolved and, since trade routes and key communication points were now better understood, the French and the Company, with Captain Lugard as their champion, manoeuvred for position. In retrospect the contest has its comic side with Lugard and his rival, Captain Decœur, literally racing to conclude treaties with important chiefs first. But it was also dangerous. The French advance had always been a military one. The British government now allowed the Company to set up the West Africa Frontier Force, under Lugard (90). It seemed inevitable that, sooner or later, a serious clash would occur. So far the European powers had avoided any military confrontation among themselves during the whole partition of Africa. The British Prime Minister, Salisbury, was determined that one should not occur now. His Colonial Secretary, Joseph Chamberlain, was by now interested in West Africa for its own sake. It was one of the many 'undeveloped estates' (136) which Britain had acquired in Africa which must be financed and administered efficiently so that they ceased to be a financial burden and became a great economic asset to the empire as a whole. He was disposed to argue the case in detail and attach importance to retaining a number of crucial positions. Salisbury, however, saw the details of a West African settlement as subordinate to his more general African strategy. To Salisbury at this time the Niger was less important than the Nile. In the event a Niger boundary settlement, reasonably acceptable to all parties, was agreed in June 1898 (26, 39, 41).

A few months later all interest shifted to the Nile with the famous 'Fashoda incident'. The status of the Sudan in international law was unclear after the Egyptian evacuation of 1885. The British held that the area still belonged to the Egyptians although they were temporarily prevented from exercising jurisdiction there. The French on the other hand held that it had become *res nullius* with no internationally recognised government. This implied that it was open to seizure by the first comer [doc. 22]. After 1887 the British had resigned themselves to the fact that they were the government of Egypt for the foreseeable future. They did not want to see any other power in control of the Upper Nile. Controversy raged then as it has raged since as to whether any occupying power in the Sudan could have diverted the course of the Nile and so made Britain's position in Egypt untenable. Very possibly the risk was chimerical but it was one that the War Office preferred not to have to face. Moreover, the death of Gordon was still unavenged. That tragedy, however, to some extent cut both ways for no one could doubt that the reconquest of the Sudan would be a serious undertaking that might cost a great deal in money and lives (27, 41, 70, 101).

The British government did not take any steps towards a reconquest until a foreign threat seemed imminent. Just as some Englishmen dreamt of an all British route from the Cape to Cairo so some Frenchmen began to plan for an all French route from west to east, from Senegal to the Red Sea. In 1893 this took a more definite form in projects for missions first by Major Monteil and subsequently by Major Liotard from the Ubanghi to the Upper Nile. Liotard consolidated French authority on the Upper Ubanghi but it was another French officer, Major Marchand, who between 1896 and 1898 made an epic overland journey from the Congo to Fashoda, a small outpost on the Upper Nile above Khartoum [doc. 22] (20). Already in 1895 Sir Edward Grey, then Under Secretary at the Foreign Office, had warned the French that any encroachment on the Upper Nile would be regarded as an 'unfriendly act' by the British government (42, 62). By now Britain had reason to be worried. The Italians had tried to establish a protectorate over Abyssinia. They had been severely defeated at the battle of Adowa in March 1896. The British did not object to an Italian presence in Abyssinia – they had gone some way to recognising it by an agreement of 1890 – and they were disturbed by the fact that the Abyssinians had had some backing from France. The plight of Italian nationals cut off at Kassala in 1896 gave the British a rather transparent excuse to re-enter the Sudan. In fact there is no doubt that this was part of a carefully conceived strategy by Salisbury to make the Upper Nile safe once and for all (41). The campaign was entrusted to General Kitchener who was already familiar with the area. Kitchener advanced with great caution, securing his communications at each step by building a railway (see p.

70 above). His ·tactics paid. When he finally met the Dervishes at the great battle of Omdurman in September 1898 he won a decisive victory (**27, 70**). The Sudan was now safe for Britain although legal complications remained. The British government had been careful to instruct Kitchener to act always in the name of the Egyptian government and Kitchener had made this clear to all by flying the British and Egyptian flags side by side [**doc. 22a**]. (It is worth noting in passing, since the Egyptians have not generally enjoyed a good reputation as fighters in the twentieth century, that a large part of Kitchener's army was Egyptian, the army built up by Sir Evelyn Wood, Field Marshall Lord Grenfell and Kitchener himself after Arabi's defeat.) The French, however, were still reluctant to admit the continuing validity of the Egyptian claim and, after the battle of Omdurman, the British decided to put their claim on the simpler ground, incontrovertible in international law, of right of conquest. A few days after the battle of Omdurman Kitchener found Marchand and his small beleaguered force at Fashoda. Very properly, the two men exchanged courtesies and referred the diplomatic questions to their governments. The excitement in the two capitals was intense. There was talk of war, even some preparation of fleets. But, in the end, realism prevailed in Paris. The French budget was unbalanced, her army in disarray after the Dreyfus scandal. Britain had presented her with a *fait accompli* in the Sudan. The French gave in and signed an agreement with Britain in March 1899 which left Britain in complete control of the Sudan (**41, 70**).

Some doubt exists whether the Fashoda crisis hindered or helped a final understanding between Britain and France about colonial matters. The man who became French Foreign Minister in the middle of the crisis, Théophile Delcassé (who, ironically, had been one of the originators of the Monteil mission) argued that it delayed for some years the reconciliation with England that he so much desired (**20**). This may be true but it can equally well be argued that it finally cleared the air between them. The partition of Africa was now virtually complete. The French were compelled to admit that the British position in Egypt seemed for the time impregnable. This opened the way for the growing lobby in France who wished to cut their losses in Egypt and concentrate on securing Morocco to complete their West African empire. The Colonial Secretary, Eugene Étienne, was among their number and, in April 1904, after two years of negotiations, a whole series of colonial bargains were signed between England and France. Some did not relate to Africa at all but the crux of the agreements was the bargain struck over Egypt and Morocco. The French would cease to obstruct British administration in Egypt and the British would withdraw any objection to the establishment of French influence in Morocco [**doc. 23**]. West African boundaries were slightly adjusted in return for French concessions in other parts of the world (**78, 114**).

The 1904 agreements were very valuable to Britain. She could at last move freely in Egypt. The British consul-general, Lord Cromer, had indeed brought strong pressure to bear on the British Foreign Office to settle with France on almost any terms lest the Egyptian finances break down altogether. But the real importance of the agreements was long term. On paper they were merely a series of colonial bargains. Only on a few very limited questions concerning Egypt and Morocco did they even commit the two powers to act together. They certainly did not constitute even an *entente* in European diplomatic terms. What turned them into something much more important were the clumsy German attempts to probe into their meaning and the German challenge to the Anglo-French agreement in Morocco, which led first to the Algeciras Conference of 1906 and later to the Agadir incident of 1911. The French were not able to make good their claim to Morocco until 1912, but in the meantime their relations with Britain had become closer and closer (**42, 78, 105**).

Britain entered the war of 1914 on the side of France and Russia, her two main colonial rivals, against Austria and Germany. With Austria she had had no colonial quarrels, with Germany comparatively few. This fact in itself must raise doubts as to whether the 'new imperialism' of the late nineteenth century did, as Hobson maintained, distort the diplomatic alignments of Europe (**117**). Lenin's contention that the First World War was an 'imperialist war' was a different point altogether. He believed that the war resulted from the attempted redistribution of territories under 'imperialist' control, defining this to include economic as well as political control, and referring to European and Turkish lands. The swallowing of Africa and large parts of Asia by the European powers was a mere *aperitif* to this movement. The theories are often confused but the issue is clearly set out in a very important article by Professor Stokes (**151**). The alignments of the First World War seem to have been determined by traditional European considerations, above all by the balance of power within that continent. Inevitably this raises the question what was the fundamental significance of the 'new imperialism' for Europe? Was it basically an economic movement or a political one, defining political in the widest possible sense to include diplomatic and strategic considerations? What were its long term results?

Africa and the Ottoman Empire in 1914

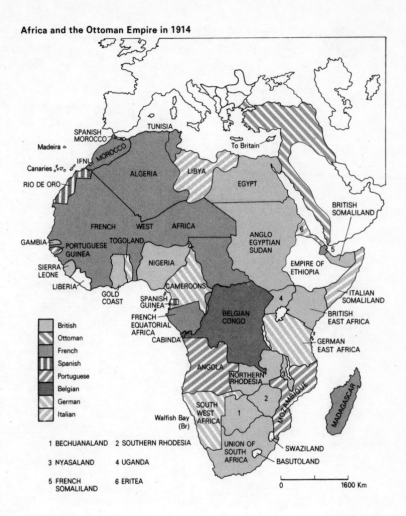

SPANISH MOROCCO
TUNISIA
Madeira
To Britain
IFNI MOROCCO
Canaries
ALGERIA
LIBYA
RIO DE ORO
EGYPT
BRITISH SOMALILAND
FRENCH WEST AFRICA
ANGLO EGYPTIAN SUDAN
GAMBIA
PORTUGUESE GUINEA
TOGOLAND
NIGERIA
EMPIRE OF ETHIOPIA
SIERRA LEONE
LIBERIA
GOLD COAST
CAMEROONS
ITALIAN SOMALILAND
SPANISH GUINEA
FRENCH EQUATORIAL AFRICA
BELGIAN CONGO
BRITISH EAST AFRICA
CABINDA
GERMAN EAST AFRICA
ANGOLA
NORTHERN RHODESIA
MOZAMBIQUE
MADAGASCAR
Walfish Bay (Br)
SOUTH WEST AFRICA
SWAZILAND
UNION OF SOUTH AFRICA
BASUTOLAND

Legend:
- British
- Ottoman
- French
- Spanish
- Portuguese
- Belgian
- German
- Italian

1 BECHUANALAND   2 SOUTHERN RHODESIA
3 NYASALAND   4 UGANDA
5 FRENCH SOMALILAND   6 ERITEA

0   1600 Km

PART THREE
Assessment

8 Conclusion

The Scramble for Africa lasted at most twenty years but, during that period, it went through a number of distinct phases. In the early and mid-1880s no European power or statesman (with the possible exception of Leopold of the Belgians) had any very clear idea of what territory they wished to acquire in Africa, or indeed whether they wished to acquire any at all. Yet, it was during this period that the most critical decisions were taken. Practically all the significant maritime powers of western Europe (with the important exception of the Dutch who were content with their possessions in the Far East) gathered into their respective 'spheres of influence' those fragments of Africa which history, or other accidental circumstances, placed within their grasp. It was done without enthusiasm. It was also done without effective political opposition at home. It was as if politicians and public alike were so taken by surprise by an unprecedented turn of events that they could not immediately formulate their attitudes.

This was particularly true in Britain. The fact that a Liberal government, under William Gladstone, was in power from 1880 to 1885 added to the confusion. Nothing would be more mistaken than to see a simple division between right (imperialist) and left (anti-imperialist) in British politics in the late nineteenth century. Both Conservatives and Liberals had been perfectly happy with the situation in the middle of the century when 'moral suasion' seemed to give Britain strong influence on both the East and the West coast of Africa without the expense and possible danger of direct intervention (96). Both Conservatives and Liberals had to face the situation after about 1870 when the rise of powerful new industrial states challenged their old-established trading supremacy. The change in British thinking can be discerned, as Bodelsen long ago realised, as early as Gladstone's first administration of 1868-74. Previously it had been fashionable to express mildly 'separatist' views, to believe that Britain's existing colonies, mainly colonies of settlement, would 'grow to maturity' and separate from the mother country in, it was hoped, an amiable and mutually agreeable manner (111). The first reaction against this was anything but extravagant and jingoistic. It represented a sober realisation that colonies might have their uses and it concerned itself almost entirely with the colonies of settlement. It found expression in the establishment of the Colonial Society (later the Royal Colonial Institute) in 1868, where eminent men were to meet to read papers and discuss questions of imperial interest. Its members represented a wide political spectrum. Lord Granville (a vice-president), Edward Cardwell and H. C. E. Childers from the Liberal side, Lord Salisbury, Lord Carnarvon and Sir Stafford Northcote from the Conservative side, were among its founders. The Society certainly had no thought of advocating an expansion of empire but, once admit that existing colonies are of value and should be defended, certain consequences begin to flow. In African terms it is now clear that it was Gladstone's government of 1868-74, not their Conservative successors, who inaugurated a forward policy on the Gold Coast. The Conservatives were responsible for the British forward policy in South Africa but they subsequently maintained, with some plausibility, that they had successfully pursued the old policy of 'influence' in Egypt, with French cooperation, in the 1870s and that it had been Liberal blunders which led to the breakdown of that policy in the 1880s. In West and East Africa and as far south as Bechuanaland it was Gladstone's government which committed the country to the acquisition of spheres of influence and 'protectorates' in the critical period 1884-86. Their reluctance and even bewilderment at this turn of events is obvious from both their official despatches and their private letters.

Similar uncertainty is discernible in France and Germany. France, like Britain, had a long colonial history but, after their decisive defeat by Germany in 1871, Frenchmen were deeply divided between those who wished to seek compensation overseas and those who saw overseas adventures as a distraction from the reassertion of their true role in Europe. Some like Camille Pelletan lamented 'Alsace-Lorraine is under the Prussian jackboot and our army is leaving for Tonkin'. Some saw all overseas commitments as a Bismarckian trap into which France must not fall. But a colonial lobby can be identified even in the 1880s. Jules Ferry, himself a Lorrainer, defended the French advance in Tunis and in Indo-China. Freycinet was much more interested in grandiose schemes for West Africa than has hitherto been realised. Army and navy officers were active in both West Africa and Indo-China. But the French public was by no means convinced in the mid-1880s. When things went wrong in Tunis in 1881 or in Tonkin in 1885 governments fell and politicians' heads rolled — very nearly literally on the latter occasion (58, 114).

Germany, too, was divided. Many Germans saw their country as essentially a continental one and could generate no enthusiasm overseas adventures. Others felt that the next step to the German victory of 1871 was the establishment of Germany as a world power. A few even advocated that Germany should annex the French colonies as part of the peace settlement of 1871. They elicited little response at that time from Bismarck. But a substantial colonial lobby grew up centred on the great trading ports of Hamburg and Bremen. By 1884 Bismarck himself conceded that colonialism was a significant election issue (**40, 48, 107**).

This period of indiscriminate grab and bewildered politicians and public did not last long. Bismarck was the first to see that these new African issues could be harnessed to the general purposes of European diplomacy. Domestic pressures undoubtedly played a part in Bismarck's actions in 1884-85 but he also seized the opportunity to try, however unsuccessfully, to reach a new understanding with France (**31, 152**). In Britain Salisbury and Rosebery were men of a different stamp from Granville and Gladstone. In the late 'eighties and the 'nineties the diplomatic game in Africa took on more ordered forms, culminating in the British case with the carefully planned conquest of the Sudan. In France politicians like Hanotaux, Étienne and Delcassé had equally carefully formulated objectives that they tried with varying degrees of success to obtain.

But if governments and imperial enthusiasts began to marshal their arguments and plan their campaigns so too did the critics and opponents of imperialism. The British occupation of Egypt in 1882 occurred without effective radical opposition at home but within two years it had become the *locus classicus* of the radical charge that governments had allowed themselves to become the pawns of the financiers. One of the earliest manifestations of this was a pamphlet by Seymour Keay, *Spoiling the Egyptians: A Tale of Shame*, published in 1882. It was further developed by T. Rothstein in his *Egypt's Ruin* (1910). It was referred to by H. N. Brailsford in his *The War of Steel and Gold* (1914) and by Leonard Woolf in his *Empire and Commerce in Africa* (1920) (**98, 112, 128**). It appeared almost unchanged as late as 1959 in John Strachey's *The End of Empire* in which he asserted:

> What the British Government really wanted was that somehow or other the interest should be collected without Britain having to involve herself in the complications and responsibilities of conquering Egypt. But when it became clear that that was impossible, Britain occupied and ruled Egypt and the Soudan rather than that the bondholders should lose their money (**127**).

The Boer War was an even greater shock to British opinion and virtually brought to an end the brief popular enthusiasm for empire-building which had found expression in the Jubilee celebrations of 1897. It produced one great anti-imperialist book, J. A. Hobson's *Imperialism, a Study* (117), which is still in print seventy years later. It is significant that Hobson was a Liberal (with some socialist leanings) who was primarily interested in the social question at home. His condemnation of imperialism arose from his diagnosis of domestic economic ills. He popularised, although he did not originate, the 'surplus capital' theory of imperialism, that is that when industry produced more capital than could profitably be reinvested at home, financiers were compelled or encouraged to invest abroad. Having invested in unstable countries they demanded, successfully, that their governments should intervene, by force if necessary, to protect their investments. Hobson, however, argued that this state of surplus capital would never come about but for its twin evil of 'underconsumption'. Briefly, too great a share of the profits of industry went into too few hands. If profits were more equitably distributed through higher wages, the consumer power of the mass of the population would be greatly increased, the home market would expand again, the problem of over-production would be solved and there would be ample opportunities for further investment at home without seeking risky overseas outlets. Hobson believed that imperialism benefited only sectional interests, the financiers above all but also armament manufacturers, shipowners, some big industrial firms, the armed services and those middle-class families who could find employment for their sons in the new colonial civil service. These 'economic parasites', as he termed them, had played a confidence trick on the whole nation by persuading the public that imperialism was in the national interest, although in fact it was expensive and showed little return [doc. 24].

Lenin, on his own statement, took Hobson's work as the starting point for his own famous pamphlet, *Imperialism, the Highest Stage of Capitalism* (119). There were, however, essential differences between the two men, and it has rightly been pointed out in recent years that it is misleading to speak (as many commentators in the past have done) of the Hobson—Lenin theory of imperialism as if their arguments were the same. First, Lenin was primarily interested in the German situation, where the finance capital provided by the banks operated in a somewhat different fashion from the industrial capital, generated by industry itself, which provided the source of most British investment abroad in this period. Secondly, and more important, Hobson saw imperialism as an aberration, a malfunctioning of the capitalist system, which ought to be corrected and which could be corrected if it was properly understood. Lenin saw it as the inevitable result of the capitalist system and an important symptom of its ultimate and inescapable decay [doc. 25]. It was in this sense that he interpreted the First World War as the final 'imperialist war'.

Hobson's theories and part of Lenin's theories have gained wide acceptance, far beyond the ranks of the orthodox Left. A reaction against the view that the Scramble for Africa was essentially an economic phenomenon in which financiers played a particularly murky role set in after the Second World War. Closely examined, there are obvious errors and omissions in the traditional theories. Professor Sir Keith Hancock made a telling attack on Lenin's theory (at least as it gained general acceptance) in a lecture, 'Wealth of Colonies' (1949) in which he pointed out that the particular stage of capitalist development which Lenin associated with imperialism – that of monopolies and cartels – came after 1900, that is after the Scramble for Africa was complete. The answer to this may be the one indicated by Professor Stokes, that Lenin himself saw the partition of Africa and Asia as a mere preliminary to the mature imperialism manifest in the First World War (51), but Lenin cannot altogether escape a charge of ambiguity since he does, not infrequently, in his pamphlet refer to events in Africa or Asia as examples of imperialism. In an article in the *Economic History Review* (133) D. K. Fieldhouse gathered together and analysed an impressive array of arguments casting doubt on financial explanations of the 'new imperialism'. If such explanations were correct, he argued, one would expect a clear correlation between financial involvement and new annexations. No such correlation exists. On the contrary, 'the places now to be taken over had hitherto attracted little capital, and did not attract it in any quantity subsequently'. There was undoubtedly considerable investment abroad by all the European powers, and above all by Britain in this period, but most of this went to traditional investment areas, like the United States where there was no question of political control. The whole German investment in Africa before 1914 amounted to only two-thirds of their investment in Austria–Hungary. Professor D. C. M. Platt has questioned whether individual financiers had any more influence on the British Foreign Office at the end of the nineteenth century than they did on Palmerston's Foreign Office or Cobden's Board of Trade. The Foreign Office, he maintains, had narrowly defined the circumstances in which the government would assist overseas investors and it adhered rigidly to these (144).

A number of writers since the Second World War have not contented themselves with exposing the weaknesses in the older interpretations but have offered alternative theories of their own. D. K. Fieldhouse sees the new imperialism as a natural outcome of the militant nationalism which came to dominate Europe after the victory of Bismarck's blood and iron policy in the Franco-Prussian War. This allows for a considerable psychological element. Empire was a popular cause and this 'ideological fervour [was the] natural outcome of this fevered nationalism, not the artifact of vested economic interests' (133). Further, it was one consequence of the tight alliance system that Bismarck imposed upon Europe – the system which caused Professor Medlicott to conclude that Bismarck 'made a deadlock and called it peace' (76). Fieldhouse suggests: 'Imperialism may best be seen as the extension into the periphery of the political struggle in Europe. At the centre the balance was so nicely adjusted that no positive action, no major change in the status or territory of either side was possible. Colonies thus became a means out of the impasse.'

Professors Robinson and Gallagher have put forward an even more specific explanation of the strange phenomenon of the Scramble for Africa. They are certainly not unaware of an economic dimension to the struggle but in their view 'as an explanation of European rule in tropical Africa, the theory of economic imperialism puts the trade before the flag, the capital before the conquest, the cart before the horse'. From one point of view the Scramble could be seen as a great extension of the Eastern Question. Defending her traditional interest in the route to India, Britain stumbled into Egypt in 1882. This caused a breakdown of her longstanding 'gentleman's agreement' with France on their respective spheres in West Africa. Concern for her route to India also compelled Britain to defend her established position in South Africa and to undertake new commitments in East Africa. Only after Africa had been partitioned for strategic reasons did the British government try to develop their sphere economically and the British public try to convince themselves that what they had done was a good thing (96). Robinson and Gallagher go further and suggest that the whole partition of Africa was 'a remarkable freak'. It was always an aberration and the surprising thing is not that it collapsed in three-quarters of a century but that it survived so long. 'It would be a gullible historiography', they conclude, 'which could see such gimcrack creations as necessary functions of the balance of power or as the highest stage of capitalism.' They also raise the important question of the role of the Africans and believe, 'the crucial changes that set all working took place in Africa itself. . . . The last quarter of the century has often been called the "Age of Imperialism". Yet much of this imperialism was no more than an involuntary reaction of Europe to the various proto-nationalisms of Islam' [doc. 27] (146).

Has the wheel come full circle and economic explanations of the Scramble been superseded by political ones? This would be a rash conclusion. D. C. M. Platt suggests, 'There is much in late-Victorian imperial expansion which cannot be explained by economic factors. But there is much which can' (**144**). This seems a reasonable proposition. The objections to wholly economic explanations raised in the last twenty years are cogent ones. Particular 'case histories' examined in detail reveal motives other than economic. But against that must be set the fact that contemporaries saw imperialism very largely in economic terms [docs 12, 17]: 1871 did see the triumph of militant nationalism in Europe but there was a strong economic dimension to that. For the first time in history one had a number of highly industrialised powers in a situation of cutthroat competition. Many were returning to protectionist policies. Politicians were particularly nervous ·and business confidence badly undermined by the widespread and little understood phenomenon of the 'Great Depression'. Every instinct of the business men seemed to be to grab their markets and their sources of raw material while they could. Politicians dared not resist. They were partially convinced too. So was the general public.

It is not easy to quantify, but the evidence seems to suggest that the working classes had (as both Hobson and Lenin allow) been won for the imperial cause. Hobson and Lenin saw this support as the result of a confidence trick on the part of the tiny minority who were likely actually to benefit by imperialism. This is possible. But it is also possible that there was among the working classes a hard-headed appreciation of the dangers threatening the ordinary worker in the new situation of international competition. It was easier for the investor to switch his investments than for the Lancashire cotton operative to find new employment if the British textile industry lost its markets. Hobson began with an examination of the social problem at home and came to the conclusion that imperialism was a false answer. Other men began with a similar preoccupation with domestic problems – Joseph Chamberlain in Britain, Friedrich Fabri in Germany, for example – and concluded that empire building was the only safe way out. They did not expect immediate returns. They were 'pegging out claims for posterity', safeguarding 'undeveloped estates'. For a generation they were, on the whole, believed. Imperialism became, as Fieldhouse says, 'the ideology of millions'.

Imperialism was believed to be right in the sense that it was in the national interest. It was believed to be right in other ways too. It was benefiting the 'backward' native, bringing him up to the standards of western civilisation. This made imperialism attractive to many liberals and humanitarians. A number of Fabians, including Bernard Shaw and y Webb, saw great possibilities for good in imperialism, as well as many things to be criticised (126). Imperialism was accepted as right in a third way too. Although some intellectuals raised doubts, most people in the late nineteenth century accepted the idea of progress in human affairs as self-evident. Theories of evolution were generally applied to societies. Western societies were further advanced than African or Asian societies. It was both proper and inevitable that the more advanced would conquer and rule the less advanced. In the end it would be to the advantage of both. But above all it was inescapable. Many imperialists — Cecil Rhodes was perhaps the most striking example — felt that they were in tune with the *Zeitgeist*, the spirit of history, and this gave them both a comforting assurance that they were on the winning side and a kind of absolution for any dubious acts they might have to commit in fulfilling an inevitable and ultimately benevolent destiny [doc. 19b].

But where in all this did the African stand? Did he, as Professors Robinson and Gallagher among others have suggested, play an active role in the remaking of Africa in the nineteenth century? (146) Was he doomed to form a new proletariat on which even the European working classes could batten as a *rentier* class, as Lenin supposed? (119). Did he gain from contact with the more 'advanced' west, as men like Lugard and Cromer hoped? [doc. 26]. Clearly Africans were not passive, was at one time supposed, in the nineteenth century. They were peoples with a long history who had already held the Europeans at bay for centuries. In the short run, however, the imbalance of technological power was so great that the political decisions of the late nineteenth century do seem to have been those of the Europeans. Even the most casual glance at the modern map of Africa reveals those straight state boundaries along lines of latitude and longitude which were clearly drawn in the chancelleries of Europe and bore little relationship to African conditions. On the other hand it is true that Islam, originally a foreign importation but one which the Africans had long ago made their own, began a period of revival in the late nineteenth century (16). Sometimes this reinforced political resistance to the European invader as in Algeria, Egypt, the Egyptian Sudan or the emirates of the Western Soudan which fought hard against the French advance. Essentially however, when the Africans sufficiently rallied their forces to throw off the foreign yoke — which they did within a century of the conquest — they fought their conquerors with their own ideological weapons. Their rallying cries were nationalism, self-determination, democracy, socialism. No doubt at least the last three of these had existed in their own forms in African societies in the past but it would be false history to suggest that, as they were formulated in the twentieth century, they did not derive directly from the west. The colonial conquests of the nineteenth century ended Africa's isolation, which had been marked in recent centuries. Rapidly, and sometimes brutally, Africa was dragged into the twentieth century. Not everything the Europeans brought was bad. Medicine and new methods of agriculture were generally good. Political ideas could be used for good or ill. But what is now clear is that in Africa, as in Asia, this was but one more layer superimposed upon an already vigorous people with a long history.

PART FOUR

Documents

THE VICTORIAN IMAGE OF AFRICA

David Livingstone: humanitarian

Livingstone, the greatest of the missionary explorers of the mid-nineteenth century commanded a wide audience at home. He was much more sympathetic to the Africans than many of his contemporaries but he saw Africa as a country 'whose history is only just beginning' and felt that the white man had a right, indeed an obligation, to change it.

It has been my object in this work to give as clear an account as I was able to of tracts of country previously unexplored, with their river systems, natural productions, and capabilities; and to bring before my countrymen, and all others interested in the cause of humanity, the misery entailed by the slave-trade in its inland phases; a subject on which I and my companions are the first who have had an opportunity of forming a judgement. . . . In our exploration the chief object in view was not to discover objects of nine days' wonder, to gaze and be gazed at by barbarians; but to note the climate, the natural productions, the local diseases, the natives and their relations to the rest of the world; all of which were observed with that peculiar interest which, as regards the future, the first white man cannot but feel in a continent whose history is only just beginning. . . . The slave-trade is the greatest obstacle in existence to civilization and commercial progress; and as the English are the most philanthropic people in the world, and will probably always have the largest commercial stake in the African continent, the policy for its suppression in every possible way shows thorough wisdom and foresight.

Most writers believe the blacks to be savages, nearly all blacks believe the whites to be cannibals. The nursery hobgoblin of the one is black, of the other white. Without going further on with these unwise comparisons, we must smile at the heaps of nonsense which have been written about the Negro intellect. When for greater effect we employ broken English, and use silly phrases as if translations of remarks, which, ten to one, were never made, we have unconsciously caricatured ourselves and not the Negroes; for it is a curious fact that Europeans almost invariably begin to speak with natives by adding the letters *e* and *o* to their words 'Give*e* me corn*o*, me give*e* you biscuit*o*' or 'Look*o*, look*o*, me want*e* beer*o* much*e*'. . . . A complaint as to the poverty of the language is often only a sure proof of the scanty attainments of the complainant. . . . In reference to the status of the Africans among the nations of the earth, we have seen nothing to justify the notion that they are of a different 'breed' or 'species' from the most civilised. The African is a man with every attribute of human kind. Centuries of barbarism have had the same deteriorating effects on Africans, as Pritchard describes them to have had on certain of the Irish who were driven some generations back, to the hills in Ulster and Connaught.

David and Charles Livingstone, *Narrative of an Expedition to the Zambesi . . . 1858-64* John Murray, 1865, pp. v, 6, 8, 67, 596.

document 2

Commerce

Livingstone believed not only that legitimate commerce would drive out the slave trade but that a rising standard of living would be the quickest way by which the Africans would attain 'civilisation'.

Pity the market is not supplied with English manufactures in exchange for the legitimate products of the country. If English merchants would come up the Zambesi during the months of June, July and August the slave trader would very soon be driven out of the market. . . .

Mr O[swell] thinks that agents or commissioners situated in different parts in that region would in the course of ten years extirpate the slave trade. . . . If it is profitable for those who are engaged in the coast trade to pass along in their ships and pick up ivory, bees wax &c., those who may have enterprise enough to push into the interior and recieve [*sic*] the goods at first hand would surely find it more profitable. The returns of the first year might be small, but those who for the love of their species would run some risk would assuredly be no losers in the end. The natives would readily acquire the habit of saving for a market. . . . Give the people the opportunity they will civilise themselves, and that more effectually than can be done by missionary societies.

D. Livingstone, *Private Journals, 1851-53*, ed. I. Schapera, Chatto & Windus, 1960, pp. 43-4, from 'First Journey to Sebitoane's Country'.

Africa as El Dorado

Men had long thought that the interior of Africa might hold untold riches. These hopes seemed to be confirmed by the reports of sober and well-trained observers like Lieutenant Verney Lovett Cameron who had learned of the resources of Katanga on his east-west crossing of the continent in 1873-5.

Most of the country from the Tanganyika to the West Coast is one of almost unspeakable richness. Of metals, there are iron, copper, silver and gold; coal is also found; the vegetable products are palm-oil, cotton, nutmegs, besides several sorts of pepper and coffee, all growing wild. The people cultivate several other oil-producing plants, such as ground-nuts and seni seni. The Arabs, as far as they have come, have introduced rice, wheat, onions, and a few fruit trees, all of which seem to flourish well. The countries of Bihé and Bailunda are sufficiently high above the sea to be admirably adapted for European occupation, and would produce whatever may be grown in the south of Europe. The oranges which Señor Goncalves [a Portuguese merchant with whom Cameron had stayed] had planted at Bihé . . . were finer than any I had ever seen in Spain or Italy. He also had roses and grapes growing in luxuriance. . . . To the eastward of Lovalé ivory is marvellously plentiful. The price among the Arab traders at Nyangwé was 7½ pounds of beads, or 5 pounds of cowries, for 35 pounds of ivory; and the caravans that went out from there for ivory would obtain tusks, irrespective of weight, for an old knife, a copper bracelet, or any other useless thing which might take the fancy of the natives.

Lieutenant Cameron's report to the Royal Geographical Society, April 1876; *Proceedings of the Royal Geographical Society*, 1st ser., xx, 323-4.

Darkest Africa: fully developed racism

H. H. Johnston had extensive experience of tropical Africa, East and West, both as an explorer and as an administrator. He had no doubts about the backwardness of the Negro races. In 1920 he drew up a kind of league table of the nations of the world. Britain, the United States and most countries of western Europe were in the first division; the countries of tropical Africa in the fifth, sixth and seventh divisions.

[a] The chief and obvious distinction between the backward and the forward peoples is that the former, with the exception of about 20,000,000 in the Mediterranean basin and the Near East, are of coloured skin; while the latter are white-skinned or, as in the case of the Japanese and the inhabitants of Northern China, nearly white.

H. H. Johnston, *The Backward Peoples and Our Relations with Them*, Oxford University Press, 1920, pp. 7-9.

Johnston held that the Negro had only himself to blame for his condition.

[b] Yet about the African slave trade, as with most other instinctive human procedure, and the movements of one race against another, there is an underlying sense of justice. The White and Yellow peoples have been the unconscious agents of the Power behind Nature in punishing the Negro for his lazy backwardness. ... The races that will not work persistently and doggedly are trampled on, and in time displaced, by those who do.

H. H. Johnston, *A History of the Colonization of Africa by Alien Races*, Cambridge University Press, 1913.

But even Johnston did not think that the Negro's condition was hopeless.

[c] There are many tribes of Negroes of the present day who are leading lives not much superior in intellectual advancement to those of the brutes; but there is not an existing race of man in Africa that is not emphatically human and capable of improvement.

Quoted [87], p. 351.

On the contrary he warned his fellow white man that the situation might change very rapidly.

[d] But the White people must try to realise that the still Backward races, the once decrepit nations, have travelled far in intellectuality since the middle of the nineteenth century, and that the continuance of an insulting policy towards them will join them some day in a vast league against Europe and America, which will set back the millenium and perhaps even ruin humanity in general.

The Backward Peoples and Our Relations with Them, p. 61.

document 5

Stanley's antipathy

Johnston's racism was tempered by a strong sense of responsibility, not so that of H. M. Stanley who, by the end of his career in Africa, scarcely seems to have regarded the inhabitants as human. The following is from his account of the Enim Pasha rescue expedition.

On the 12th December we left camp at dawn without disturbance, or hearing a single voice, and up to 9 a.m. it did not appear as if anybody was astir throughout the valley. Our road lead E. by S. and dipped down into ravines, and narrow valleys, down which its tributaries from the mountain range and its many gorges flowed under depths of jungle, bush and reed-cane. Villages were seen nestling amid abundance, and we left them unmolested in the hope that the wild people might read that when left alone we were an extremely inoffensive band of men. But at nine o'clock . . . we heard the first war-cries. . . . By 11 a.m. there were two separate bands of natives who followed us very persistently. One had come from the eastward, the other was formed out of the population of the villages in the valley that we had left undamaged and intact [*after a previous skirmish*] .

By noon these bands had increased into numerous and frantic mobs, and some of them cried out, 'We will prove to you before night that we are men, and every one of you shall perish today . . . .' The mobs followed us, now and then making demonstrations, and annoying us with their harsh cries and menaces. An expert shot left the line of march, and wounded two of them at a range of 400 yards. This silenced them for a while. . . .

Finally at 3.30, we came in view of the Bavira villages situated on an open plain and occupying both banks of a deep and precipitous ravine hollowed out of the clay by a considerable tributary of the East Ituri. [*The natives tried to prevent the party crossing the river.*] Loads were at once dropped . . . and a smart scene of battle-play occurred, at the end of which the natives retreated on the full run. To punish them for four hours persecution of us we turned about and set fire to every hut on either bank. . . . It should be observed that up to the moment of firing the villages, the fury of the natives seemed to be increasing, but the instant the flames were seen devouring their homes the fury ceased, by which we learned that fire had a remarkable sedative influence on their nerves.

H. M. Stanley, *In Darkest Africa*, London, 1890, i, pp. 299-300.

EGYPT

document 6

Suez Canal

[a] *Sir Charles Dilke's speech in the House of Commons, 25 July 1882.*

Egypt forms our highway to India and to the East generally. . . . As regards the Suez Canal, England has a double interest; it has a predominant commercial interest, because 82 per cent of the trade passing through the Canal is British trade, and it has a predominant political interest caused by the fact that the Canal is the principal highway to India, Ceylon, the Straits and British Burmah, where 250,000,000 people live under our rule; and also to China, where we have vast interests and 84 per cent of the external trade of that still more enormous Empire It is also one of the roads to our Colonial Empire in Australia and New Zealand.

Hansard, 3rd ser. vol. 272, 1720.

[b] *J. C. M'Coan (Liberal M.P. for Co. Wicklow) in the same debate.*

The Suez Canal was of paramount and national importance to England; indeed, it was a common thing to say that it formed the gate and key to India. So long, therefore, as we held the Empire of India, we must of necessity, dominate the Suez Canal.

Ibid. 1758.

[c] *Henry Labouchère (Radical M.P. for Northampton) in the same debate, 27 July 1882.*

He considered it absolutely necessary to maintain a supreme and paramount influence over the Canal, and that it was impossible to maintain that influence unless we also had paramount influence at Cairo.

Ibid. 2050-1.

Dissident views

[d] *William Gladstone in August 1877*

Suppose the very worst. The Canal is stopped [*by Russian action*]. And what then? A heavy blow will have been inflicted on the commerce of the world. We, as the great carriers, and as the first commercial nation of Christendom, shall be the greatest losers. But it is a question of loss and of loss only. . . . What came and went quickly and cheaply must come and go slow and dearer. . . . I turn then to the military question and ask how much Russia will have gained? The answer is, that she will have introduced an average delay of about three weeks into our military communications with Bombay and less with Calcutta. It seems to be forgotten by many, that there is a route to India round the Cape of Good Hope, as completely as if that route lay by the North-west Passage. [Three weeks delay] will hardly make the difference to us between life and death in the maintenance of our Indian Empire.

The Nineteenth Century, ii (1877), 155-6.

[e] *Lord Randolph Churchill's speech at Edinburgh, 18 December 1883*

Egypt is not the high road to India. The Suez Canal is a commercial route to India, and a good route too, in time of peace: but it never was, and never could be, a military route for Great Britain in time of war.

L. J. Jennings, *Speeches of Rt. Hon. Randolph Churchill*, 1880-88, i, 74: extracts in W. S. Churchill, *Lord Randolph Churchill*, pp. 219-20.

document 7

The Egyptian Finances: Stephen Cave's Report

The critical state of the finances of Egypt is due to the combination of two opposite causes.

Egypt may be said to be in a transition state, and she suffers from the defects of the system out of which she is passing, as well as from those of the system into which she is attempting to enter. She suffers from the ignorance, dishonesty, waste, and extravagance of the East, such as have brought her Suzerain [*the Sultan of Turkey*] to the verge of ruin, and at the same time from the vast expense caused by hasty and inconsiderate endeavours to adopt the civilization of the West.

Immense sums are expended on unproductive works after the manner of the East, and on productive works carried out in the wrong way, or too soon. This last is a fault which Egypt shares with other new countries (for she may be considered a new country in this respect) a fault which has seriously embarrassed both the United States and Canada; but probably nothing in Egypt has ever approached the profligate expenditure which characterized the commencement of the Railway system in England.

[Fundamentally, Cave found the Egyptian economy sound. The Egyptian revenue had risen from £55,000 in 1804 to £7,377,912 in 1871. If one compared the two periods, 1850-62 and 1863-75; imports had doubled and exports quadrupled – the latter from £36,339,543 to £145,939,736. The population was rising. There had been a great drive for

education. In 1862 there had been only 185 European-type schools, in 1875 there were 4,817. Although mistakes had been made in building up the Egyptian cotton and sugar industries — for example siting factories in the wrong place — the potential was great.]

The expenditure, though heavy, would not of itself have produced the present crisis, which may be attributed almost entirely to the ruinous conditions of loans raised for pressing requirements. . . .

In 1862 Said Pasha contracted the first loan. The nominal amount was £3,292,800, repayable in thirty years; the interest 7 per cent and the sinking fund 1 per cent. We have no particulars of the amount really received on this loan.

In 1864 the first of the present Viceroy's [*Ismail*] loans was contracted. The nominal amount was £5,704,200, of which, however, only £4,864,063 was received. The interest and sinking fund on the nominal amount were respectively 7 and 3.87 per cent, but on the amount received they were 8.2 and 4.5, or, together, 12.7 per cent, instead of 10.87 per cent on the nominal value.

[*Similar real interest rates were exacted on the loans of 1868 and 1873 but the worst examples of extortion was the railway loan of 1866.*]

A loan was raised for the construction of railways in 1866. Its nominal amount was £3,000,000 at 7 per cent. The amount received by the State was £2,640,000, which raised the interest to 8 per cent. The full amount of £3,000,000 was repaid by six annual instalments of £500,000 each, from 1 January 1869, to 1 January 1874, a rate equivalent to a sinking fund of 18.9 per cent; so that during six years this loan entailed on the State an average charge of equal to 26.9 per cent of the amount realized.

[*After various technical proposals for ameliorating the situation Cave concluded.*]

It would appear from these calculations that the resources of Egypt are sufficient, if properly managed, to meet her liabilities, but that as all her available assets are pledged for the charges of existing loans, some fresh combination is necessary in order to fund at a moderate rate the present onerous floating debt.

[Cave was prepared to see a European official brought in to control the levying of taxation. He was aware that the increasing employment of European officials was a source of criticism but his own views, expressed earlier in his Report were:]

They would be checks upon the adventurers who have preyed upon Egypt. . . . An official of high rank said to us that the great want in Egypt is a body of high-class Europeans, not those who compete with each other to make money, and put pressure upon the Khedive, but men like our Indian officials, who have done so much to raise the tone of the native races.

Report by Mr Cave on the Financial Condition of Egypt, 23 March 1876, *Parliamentary Papers*, lxxxiii (1876), 99.

document 8

Divided opinions

[a] *Joseph Chamberlain's memorandum*

I think that Liberal opinion in the country will be extremely restive at the idea of armed intervention either for the maintenance of the [Anglo-French] Control in the interests of the bondholders or for the enforcement of restrictions on the right of the Egyptian people to manage their own affairs. [No doubt the Control has done good work] but if the people of Egypt prefer native administration with all its consequences to the inflexible security and honesty of European control, it is not England's business or right to force on them an unpopular system which could only be permanently maintained against their wishes by practically assuming the Government of the country. On the other hand, if a change is to be made in a system which has the sanction of International agreement it should be on the demand of some body entitled to speak for the Egyptian people, and not at the dictation of a military adventurer supported by an army which he is forced to keep in a good temper by bribes of pay and promotion, and whose action compromises the welfare and liberties of the people as well as the interests of foreigners. The Notables have shown some independence and seem to be the nucleus of a really national and patriotic party. Should not intervention, whether by the Sultan or anyone else, have for its chief object the liberation of this body from the military tyranny to which they have been subjected — with the understanding that any recommendations it may make for revision of existing institutions will be favourably considered?

Memorandum for the Cabinet, 21 June 1882, Joseph Chamberlain Papers, File 7/1/3, Birmingham University Library. Cf. extracts in Garvin [39], i, 448.

[b] *Evelyn Baring to Lord Northbrook, 27 March 1882*

It does not seem to me that we ought to interfere *vi et armis* because the Egyptians want to levy their taxes, vote their Budget etc. etc. in a different way to that which at present obtained. I daresay the movement may not now be thoroughly national, but I should think it would become so directly we begin to suppress it by force.

Granville Papers, Public Record Office, P.R.O. 30/29/138.

[c] *Frederic Harrison at a meeting of the Anti-Aggression League, 26 June 1882.*

When two years ago, the great appeal to the nation was made, we thought it was decided for ever that England should renounce the policy of injustice, and cease to undertake the control of half the human race in the name of civilisation in general and Great Britain in particular. We were all, perhaps, a little too confident that the policy we rejected was really abandoned. . . . Tell those who are so eager to govern Arabs, and Africans, and Afghans, and Japanese at modest stipends of £4,000 or £5,000 a year — ask them to see what can be done in the better government of our own island. . . . Tell those noisy philanthropists who call heaven and earth to witness of the 'anarchy' on the Nile . . . tell them to go and do something to prevent anarchy in Ireland. . . . Imagine your own feelings, if you had to send every year some forty million sterling out of the taxes of the country to pay Turkish, or Arab, or Chinese bond-holders; and then, having paid that regularly, that you had to keep a Turkish pasha and a Chinese mandarin in London to control your expenditure, so that every penny of the Budget had to get the sanction of their excellencies, and if Mr Gladstone or any other Chancellor of the Exchequer wishes to put on or take off a tax, down would come a fleet of iron-clads from the Bosphorus into the Thames, and train their 80 ton guns right in view of the Tower and Somerset House. That is the state of Egypt now.

F. Harrison, *The Crisis in Egypt* (Anti-Aggression League Pamphlet, no. 2), pp. 3, 7, 11.

[d] *Lord Randolph Churchill, speech at Blackpool, 24 January 1884*

... The Suez Canal was at no time in the smallest danger. The Suez Canal will always take care of itself. The whole world, the East and the West, are equally and mutually interested in the freedom of the Suez Canal. Surely, you will not be misled by such an obvious and transparent fiction. It was bonds and bondholders and no other power which diverted Mr Gladstone, greatly hesitating, from his path, and which drew the British fleet to Alexandria. It was bonds and bondholders only which commanded the British troops. I pray you mark this. England has never before interfered with the internal affairs of other nations on account of bonds or debts which might be owing to her people. We have always looked upon these matters as altogether outside the range of active Government interference. The Southern States of America took a lot of money from us which they never paid. Did we go to war with the United States? ... I am afraid to say how many people in this country lost their all when Turkey repudiated her debts. The Government of England took no action. It has been left for Mr Gladstone's Government to depart from this wise and time-honoured tradition — for this Government, whose cardinal principle of foreign policy was non-intervention; it has been left for them to intervene, and intervene actively and violently, and on the

114

side of oppression as against the cause of freedom, in the one particular sphere in which till now non-intervention had been acquiesced in by both parties in the State.

L. J. Jennings, ed., *Speeches of the Rt. Hon. Lord Randolph Churchill, M.P., 1880-1888*, Longmans, 1889, i, 100.

document 9

Egypt in international diplomacy

[a] *Lord Salisbury to Sir Stafford Northcote, 16 September 1881*

As to our policy -- the defence of it lies in a nutshell. When you have got a neighbour and faithful ally who is bent on meddling in a country in which you are deeply interested -- you have three courses open to you. You may renounce -- or monopolise -- or share. Renouncing would have been to place the French across our road to India. Monopolising would have been very near the risk of war. So we resolved to share.

Cecil (**26**), ii, 331-2.

[b] *William Gladstone to the Queen, 2 February 1882*

In the matter of Egypt it appeared to the Cabinet advisable that Lord Granville should endeavour to draw off the French Government from the idea of an Anglo-French occupation, on account of the likelihood of its raising European difficulties; and should suggest to them the expediency of seeking the aid of the Powers in meeting any serious crisis which may be impending, without prejudice to the subsisting Control; and even the possibility of being found the least perilous method of using force, if unhappily force should be required, that Turkey should be employed as the instrument for giving effect to the general will.

Public Record Office, CAB 41/16

115

[c] *Lord Granville to the British Ambassadors at Berlin, Vienna, Rome and St Petersburg, 11 February 1882*

Her Majesty's Government are now agreed with the Government of France that, in view of events which might occur in Egypt, it is desirable to ascertain whether the other Powers would be willing to enter upon an exchange of views as to the best mode of dealing with the question on the basis of the maintenance of the rights of the Sovereign and of the Khedive; of international engagements and the arrangements existing under them, whether with England and France alone or with those two nations and the other Powers; the preservation of the liberties secured by the Firman of the Sultan; together with the prudent development of Egyptian institutions.

The Governments of England and France do not consider that a case for discussing the expediency of an intervention has at present arisen, since on the part of the Chamber of Notables and of the new Government the intention is avowed to maintain international engagements; but should the case arise, they would wish that any such eventual intervention should represent the united action and authority of Europe.

In that event it would also, in their opinion, be right that the Sultan should be a party to any proceeding or discussion that might ensue.

Public Record Office, F.O., *Confidential Print*, 4692, F.O. 407/19.

[d] *Lord Hartington to Lord Granville, 30 May 1882*

The French seem to be behaving worse than badly. Freycinet's communication to Ld Lyons [*the British ambassador in Paris*] appears to be nothing less than a breach of faith to us; and practically a deception of the Khedive, who will inevitably be killed before English and French troops can possibly intervene. Of course this strengthens my opinion of yesterday that unless the French keep their word to us and are prepared to go in for Turkish intervention at once, we had much better cut ourselves loose from them. What is the use of such allies? They have brought us into the frightful mess we are in, and I believe it would be easier to act with the Turks and the whole of the remaining European Powers, than with them alone.

Granville Papers, Public Record Office, P.R.O. 30/29/132.

[e] *Lord Ampthill (British Ambassador in Berlin) to Lord Granville, 15 July 1882.*

Let me congratulate you most sincerely and heartily on having so tactfully steered out of the inevitable complications of 'entangling alliances' into the independent prosecution of a truly British national policy. Everybody I meet seems overjoyed that we are asserting our right to protect our own interests, and have taken the lead of the concert into our own hands. Everybody congratulates me on your policy, with the exception of my French colleague, who is quite broken down with disappointment at Freycinet's weakness, and the absence of national pride in the French Chambers. Münster [*the German ambassador in London*] is probably right in thinking that Bismarck will now be reticent and reserved. Hatzfeldt [*formerly the German Ambassador at Constantinople*] tells me that Bismarck becomes simply furious at the mere mention of the Egyptian question, and will scarcely even read what is sent to him on the subject. 'Let the Powers interested settle it as they please [he writes to Hatzfeldt], but don't ask me *how*; for I neither know nor care' . . . . Bismarck, I think, will support any action we take, but will refrain from advice, however much he may wish England to go ahead, and settle the question as you think best for Europe.

Fitzmaurice (35), ii, 268-9.

document 10

Death of Gordon at Khartoum

[a] *The Times, 3 May 1884*

A study of the papers contained in the Blue Book . . . must produce a general sense of shame and confusion. . . . The anxiety as to General Gordon's safety is not confined to London, or fomented by Opposition prints, as is sometimes suggested; it is discernible in the organs of all classes, those of the working men not excepted, and is plainly manifested in the North of England and Scotland, the strongholds of Liberalism.

Leading article.

[b] *The Archdeacon of Northampton*

A nation mourned a son, a true son, fallen by a death of betrayal and desertion in the cause. England wept today and felt remorse, for there was no remorse like remorse for long neglect.

The Archdeacon of Northampton preaching on the day of national mourning for Gordon, 13 March 1885, reported in *The Times*, 14 March 1885.

[c] *The Morning Post*

We cannot turn our backs upon the Mahdi and his hordes without sacrificing Egypt and shaking to its foundation our Indian Empire. Having entered on this struggle, we must go on with it; and having gone to the Soudan, we can quit it only as victors. There is only one course.

Quoted *Annual Register* (1885), pp. 20, 21.

[d] *Sir George Campbell (M.P. for Kirkcaldy), House of Commons, 23 February 1885, during the debate on the Vote of Censure on the government for its policy in the Sudan.*

He [Campbell] was one of the small band who had consistently opposed the Government policy in Egypt from the bombardment of Alexandria down to the present time. Holding, therefore, the views he did, he had heard the other day with astonishment and alarm the declaration of the

Prime Minister that it was the intention of the Government to overthrow and 'smash the Mahdi', but he was glad to say that the speech of the Prime Minister that evening had to a large extent whittled away the most dangerous portion of his previous utterances. . . . They must all feel that the reconquering of that great Empire in the heart of Africa was an enormous undertaking; and, looking to their position with France, Germany and Russia, he thought they would do well to be wise in time.

Hansard, 3rd ser., vol. 244, 1110.

[e] *J. A. Picton (M.P. for Leicester), in the same debate.*

They heard a great deal about *prestige* in various articles of the Press, and in some of the speeches delivered in that House. *Prestige* was a French word, and it seemed to him to express a very un-English idea. It might be proper for a people who, under the malignant influence of Imperialism, had been trained up to think far more of glory than of truth and right; but if, by *prestige*, Hon. Members meant reputation, he would ask whether, in this ancient Kingdom, we had much need to be nervous about our reputation?

Ibid. 1122-3.

The government survived the censure motion by only 14 votes: 302 to 288.

WEST AFRICA

document 11

The desire to abandon responsibilities

Resolved:

That it is the opinion of this Committee

1. That it is not possible to withdraw the British government, wholly or immediately, from any settlements or engagements on the West African Coast. . . .

3. That all further extension of territory or assumption of Government, or new treaties offering any protection to native tribes, would be inexpedient; and that the object of our policy should be to encourage in the natives the exercise of those qualities which may render it possible for us more and more to transfer to them the administration of all the Governments, with a view to our ultimate withdrawal from all, except, probably, Sierra Leone.

Report from the Select Committee on Africa (Western Coast), Parliamentary Papers, v (1865), iii.

document 12

The fears of British traders

[a] *The National African Company on the Niger*

Foreign annexations of any degree would, as experience teaches us, practically exclude *pro tanto*, British commerce.
   . . . we have no need to dwell at length on the importance to Great Britain of keeping open to her commerce the highway to the countries of the Central Soudan, which are both densely populated and fairly civilised, nor on the facts that this waterway was discovered by an Englishman, Lander, was opened up to trade by another Englishman, McGregor Laird, under the continued auspices of Her Majesty's Government, and has had its resources rapidly developed by (until quite recently) exclusively British capital.

G. Goldie Taubman (as he then was), Vice-Chairman of the National African Co. Ltd, to T. V. Lister, Assistant Secretary at the Foreign Office, 26 September 1883, Granville Papers, Public Record Office, P.R.O. 30/29/269.

[b] *The Liverpool traders on the Congo*

John Holt, a leading Liverpool merchant who had lived on the West Coast, wrote under the influence of reports that the French had acquired territory near Stanley Pool and that the Portuguese were extending their claims to the whole coastline from the River Loge to the River Quillo.

The effect of a Portuguese extension would be to exter-
minate the British trade existing in the absorbed territory, as
it could not exist under the grinding exactions of a protective
Customs Tariff, which would practically prohibit the importation of every manufacture of British origin. A writer who
lived for many years in Angola, and who had abundant
opportunities of witnessing the miserable state to which that
fine country had been reduced by the wretched and corrupt
system of government, represents Portuguese rule there as a
'despotic oppression that crushed the whole country under
its heel, depopulating it, and stifling any attempt at industrial
development'. . . .

France of late years has been making vigorous efforts to
extend her influence in Western Africa. . . . If France sets so
high a value on her future in Africa as to deem it wise to
extend her power, and to accept gladly the responsibilities of
an enlarged empire, and if Portugal does not shrink from the
additional cares of an increased territory, it is reasonable to
hope that England will not allow the trade at present
possessed by her to be confiscated for the benefit of protectionist competitors; but that the influence due to her by
virtue of her great colonial and trading interests in Western
Africa, which far exceed those of all other nations combined,
will be maintained, and, if necessary, her territory extended,
in order to prevent the encroachments of foreign powers
whose interests are antagonistic to those of Great Britain.

John Holt, Liverpool, to Lord Granville, 11 December 1882, Granville
Papers, Public Record Office, P.R.O. 30/29/269.

[c] *The protest against the Anglo-Portuguese Treaty of February 1884*

This Treaty has been concluded in direct opposition to the
expressed views and to the interests of British merchants and
manufacturers. . . In 1856 . . . the commerce of this country
with the native territories north of the Portuguese possessions
in Angola was of small importance but . . . during the past
five years this trade has nearly quadrupled in value. . . .
Manchester furnishes the clothes, Birmingham the iron and
brass wares, Yorkshire the woollens, London the boats and
means of navigation, and Liverpool and London the pro-

visions. . . . As yet this trade is only in its infancy; if it increases at the present rate, five years hence it will be superior to anything on the West Coast of Africa. The Portuguese see this, but they are not wise enough to see that if they come and obtain possession of the Congo, commerce, so fast growing now, cannot thrive under the disadvantages attending their rule. It is only because it is free that it thrives. . . .

Manchester Chamber of Commerce to Lord Granville, 5 March 1884, *Parliamentary Papers*, lvi (1884), 89.

[d] *The German annexation of the Cameroons*

I am requested by the Directors of this Chamber to draw your attention to the action of the German Government in the Cameroons River and its adjacent territory on the West Coast of Africa.

The Directors view with alarm and anxiety the annexation by Germany of this district, which has for many years been regarded as under British protection.

Your Lordship is probably aware that there are only two firms of German nationality trading in the Cameroons, whilst of English firms there are six. The former have traded only during the last ten or fifteen years; the English firms — or, at all events, certain of them — have been established there for thirty or forty years.

In respect, therefore, of priority of settlement, Great Britain has the preferable claim of supremacy. . . .

It is, doubtless, also within your Lordship's cognizance that the natives of the district have repeatedly applied for annexation to this country; and it is well known that they are exasperated at the action of the German Government.

The Directors of the Chamber are impressed with the belief that, when these facts are brought before the Government of His Imperial Majesty the Emperor of Germany, their pretensions will be withdrawn, not alone as an act of courtesy to a nation with whom the Germans are on friendly terms, but in respect of its just claim of prior and permanent occupation.

Should it be found, however, necessary or expedient to

allow Germany to take possession of the southern bank of the Cameroons River, it is all-important that the northern bank should continue under the protection, or be formally annexed by, Great Britain, seeing that the district of Victoria (which has already been annexed by the British), as well as the Cameroons Mountains, are on this side.

John McLaren, President, Chamber of Commerce and Manufacturers, Glasgow, to Lord Granville, 10 November 1884, *Parliamentary Papers*, lv (1884-5), 82.

document 13

The British government's reaction

[a] *The government's reluctance to act.*

The responsibilities of Her Majesty's Government on the West African Coast are already very heavy, and Lord Kimberley [*Colonial Secretary*] is of the opinion that it is very undesirable to add to them. As Lord Granville is well aware the climate of all parts of West Africa is very pestilential, and prejudicial to the life and health of Europeans. Past experience shows that the extension of British occupation would probably lead to wars with the interior tribes and heavy demands upon the British taxpayer. The question of domestic slavery and of fugitive slaves from the inland tribes, which must necessarily arise, would, in Lord Kimberley's opinion, be of themselves sufficient to deter Her Majesty's Government from undertaking such a responsibility as is proposed [*the annexation of the Cameroons*] if it can possibly be avoided.

R. G. W. Herbert (Permanent Under Secretary at the Colonial Office) to the Foreign Office, 3 May 1883, Public Record Office, F.O. 84/1654.

[b] *The permanent officials begin to become converted.*

T. V. Lister, the Assistant Under Secretary at the Foreign Office with special responsibility for African affairs, was an early convert. He is here replying to a memorandum by R. H. Meade, his opposite number of the Colonial Office who never became converted.

Everybody seems to be agreed that the occupation of any place or river by the French is almost destructive of British trade, and it is therefore of great importance to keep them out of districts which either are or might be favourable to that trade.⌐

Memorandum by T. V. Lister, 24 October 1883, Granville Papers, Public Record Office, P.R.O. 30/29/269.

document 14

The Berlin West Africa Conference lays down the 'rules' for the Scramble

Chapter I. The Congo
Article 1
The trade of all nations shall enjoy complete freedom --

1. In all the regions forming the basin of the Congo and its outlets. [*The boundaries of this area are then defined in detail.*]

2. In the maritime zone extending along the Atlantic Ocean from the Parallel situated in 2° 30′ of south latitude to the mouth of the Logé. . . .

3. In the zone stretching eastwards from the Congo Basin, as above defined to the Indian Ocean from the 5° of north latitude to the mouth of the Zambesi in the south. . . .

Article 6
All the Powers exercising sovereign rights or influence in the aforesaid territories bind themselves to watch over the preservation of the native tribes, and to care for the improvement of the conditions of their moral and material well-being, and to help in suppressing slavery, and especially the Slave Trade. They shall, without distinction of creed or nation, protect and favour all religions, scientific or charitable institutions, and undertakings created and organised for the above ends, or which aim at instructing the natives and bringing home to them the blessings of civilization.

Christian missionaries, scientists, and explorers, with their followers, property, and collections, shall likewise be the objects of special protection. . . .

Chapter V. The Niger

Article 26

The navigation of the Niger, without excepting any of its branches and outlets, is, and shall remain free for the merchant-ships of all nations equally, whether with cargo or ballast, for the transportation of goods and passengers. . . .

Chapter VI. New Occupations

Article 34

Any Power which henceforth takes possession of a tract of land on the coasts of the African Continent outside of its present possessions, or which, being hitherto without such possessions, shall acquire them, as well as the Power which assumes a protectorate there, shall accompany the respective act with a notification thereof, addressed to the other Signatory Powers of the present Act, in order to enable them, if need be, to make good any claim of their own.

Article 35

The Signatory Powers of the present Act recognize the obligations to insure the establishment of authority in the regions occupied by them on the coasts of the African continent sufficient to protect existing rights, and, as the case may be, freedom of trade and of transit under the existing conditions agreed upon.

General Act of the Berlin Conference on West Africa, signed on 26 February 1885, by the representatives of Germany, Austria, Belgium, Denmark, Spain, the United States of America, France, the United Kingdom, Italy, the Netherlands, Portugal, Russia, Sweden and Norway, and Turkey. *Parliamentary Papers*, lv (1884-5), 438.

document 15
The Royal Niger Company

The Royal Niger Company, based on the British North Borneo Company (1881), itself formed the precedent for the Imperial British East Africa Company (1888) and the Cecil Rhodes's South Africa Company (1889).

The following Charter has been granted to the National African Company (Limited), upon a Petition to Her Majesty in Council:

Whereas . . . the capital of the Company is £1,000,000, divided into 100,000 shares of £10 each [of which 97,675 shares have been subscribed for]. And that the objects of the Company . . . are . . .

To carry on business and to act as merchants, bankers, traders, commission agents, ship-owners, carriers, or in any other capacity, in the United Kingdom, Africa, or elsewhere, and to import, export, buy, sell, barter, exchange, pledge, make advances upon or otherwise deal in goods, produce, articles, and merchandize, according to the custom of merchants, or otherwise.

To form or acquire and carry on trading stations, factories, stores, and depots in Africa or elsewhere, and to purchase, lease, or otherwise acquire, carry on, develop, or improve any business, or any real or personal property in the United Kingdom, Africa, or elsewhere, or any undivided or other interest whatsoever therein respectively. . . .

And whereas the Petition further states, that the Kings, Chiefs, and other peoples of various territories in the basin of the River Niger in Africa . . . have ceded the whole of their respective territories to the Company by various Acts of Cession specified in the Schedule thereto. . . .

And whereas the petitioners further state that the Company . . . have purchased the business of all the European traders in the region aforesaid, and are now the sole European traders there and are now engaged in developing the resources of such regions, and in extending trade further into the interior.

And whereas the Petition further states that the Company . . . have, during many years past, expended large sums of money and made great exertions in and about acquiring the confidence of the said native Kings, Chiefs, and peoples, which have resulted in the said cession of territory, and large expenditure will be incurred in carrying the same into effect and discharging the obligations arising thereunder.

And whereas the Petition further states that the condition of the natives inhabiting the aforesaid territories would be materially improved, and the development of such territories and those contiguous to, and the civilization of their people would be greatly advanced if we could think fit to confer on the Company . . . authority to accept the full benefit of the several cessions aforesaid. . . .

And whereas the Petition further states . . . they would be enabled to render our dominions services of much value, and to promote the commercial prosperity of many of ' our subjects.

Now, therefore, we . . . do hereby will, ordain, grant, and declare as follows, that is to say:

Authorization to Company

1. The said National African Company (Limited) . . . is hereby authorized and empowered to hold and retain the full benefit of the several cessions aforesaid or any of them, and all rights, interests, authorities, and powers for the purposes of government, preservation of public order, protection of the said territories, or otherwise of what nature or kind soever . . . ceded to or vested in the Company . . . and to hold, use, enjoy, and exercise the same territories, lands, property, rights, interests, authorities and powers respectively for the purposes of the Company . . . and to hold, use, enjoy, and exercise the same territories, lands, property, rights, interests, authorities and powers respectively for the purposes of the Company, and on the terms of this our Charter.

[*Further clauses bound the Company to remain British, to suppress slavery, to guarantee religious freedom and to respect local laws and customs.*]

Prohibition of Monopoly

14. Nothing in this our Charter shall be deemed to authorize the Company to set up or grant any monopoly of trade . . . and there shall be no differential treatment of the subjects of any Power as to settlement or access to markets, but foreigners alike with British subjects will be subject to administrative dispositions in the interests of commerce and order.

The customs duties and charges hereby authorized shall be levied and applied solely for the purpose of defraying the necessary expenses of Government. . . .

London Gazette, 13 July 1886.

[b] Treaties with African Chiefs

There were several variants of these but the one given below, the so-called 'Treaty Form No. 5', eventually became the most widely used. 168 treaties in this particular form were signed between 16 April 1884 and 12 September 1888. In the earlier treaties the Royal Niger Company was of course called the National African Company.

We, the undersigned Chiefs of [*blank*] with the view to the bettering of the condition of our country and people, do this day cede to the Royal Niger Company (Chartered and Limited), for ever, the whole of our territory extending from [*blank*].

We also give the said Royal Niger Company . . . full power to settle all native disputes arising from any cause whatever, and we pledge ourselves not to enter into any war with other tribes without the sanction of the said Royal Niger Company. . . .

We understand that the said Royal Niger Company . . . have full power to mine, farm, and build in any portion of our country.

We bind ourselves not to have any intercourse with any strangers or foreigners except through the said Royal Niger Company. . . .

In consideration of the foregoing, the said Royal Niger Company . . . bind themselves not to interfere with any of the native laws or customs of the country, consistently with the maintenance of order and good government.

The said Royal Niger Company . . . agree to pay native owners of land a reasonable amount for any portion they may require..

The said Royal Niger Company . . . bind themselves to protect the said Chiefs from the attacks of any neighbouring aggressive tribes.

The said Royal Niger Company . . . also agree to pay the said Chiefs [*blank*] measures native value.

[*There followed the signatures of witnesses to the Chiefs' marks and a declaration by an interpreter that he had 'truly and faithfully explained the above agreement to all the Chiefs present, and they understood its meaning'.*]

Parliamentary Papers, lxiii (1899), 444.

The Great Depression

The Royal Commission appointed to inquire into the Depression of Trade and Industry, 1885-6.

Questions addressed to Chambers of Commerce, Commercial Associations and (with some changes) 'Trade Societies and other Associations representing the interests of the Working Classes'.

6. . . . can the condition of trade and industry, or that of any special trade or industry, in your district at the present time be fairly described as 'depressed'?

7. . . . If so, when did the depression begin; when did it reach its lowest point; and what are its most prominent symptoms?

13. What measures could, in your opinion, be adopted to improve the existing conditions of trade?

14. To what extent do you consider that the present condition of trade and industry in your district has been affected by the operation of any of the following causes: . . .

    (h) Foreign competition.
    (k) Foreign tariffs and bounties?

Replies

[*These were immensely varied but the majority regarded foreign tariffs as a serious problem. A significant number spoke of the need for new markets. A few wanted closer links with British colonies, for example:*]

Birmingham

6. Every trade, special and ordinary, can only be described as depressed.

7. Distinct depression began in 1876-7. Lowest period during the present year.

13. . . . The formation of a trading union between the mother country and her colonies and dependencies.

14. . . . the principal causes of the present depression [include] – Foreign competition in neutral markets, the rate of wages and hours of labour in Germany, France, Belgium, and all other manufacturing countries being lower and longer than in this country, except in America.

Barnsley

13. . . . Opening up of new markets, more particularly by cultivating closer business relations with our colonies.

Manchester

13. The opening up of new markets, and development of those already partially open to Great Britain, should be assisted by Government in every practical way. Such openings now present themselves in Africa. . . .

Parliamentary Papers, xxi (1886), 73, 75, 77, 97, 114, 227.

EAST AFRICA

document 17

The mixture of economic and strategic arguments

The business men press their case

[a] The Zanzibar dominions comprise the whole coast line of that part of East Africa lying between 10° 40′ S. Lat. and about 3° N., which included upwards of forty harbours which are mostly safe and commodious. . . .

The principal exports of the mainland are ivory, gum copal, copra, semsem, millet, hides, orchella-weed, tobacco and india-rubber; the latter was unknown to the natives as an article of commerce until about 1876, but it is now one of the most valuable exports. . . .

An analysis of the trade of 1878-9, which was an average year . . . will give an approximate estimate of the proportions of the whole trade absorbed by England. The imports for that year were £709,900 and the exports £870,350 . . . fully one-third of the import and one-half of the export trade of the Zanzibar dominions, for 1878-9, was absorbed by Great Britain. [Cheap Indian cottons are tending to drive out British manufactures in the south.] But in the richer and more populous mountain region to the north the cheaper productions find no market. There we find both clothing and ornament of the most solid character. Manchester grey and blue cottons, heavy iron, copper and brass wire are in constant demand, and beyond these, a few beads are the only articles of European manufacture accepted. The manufactures, in short, which are suited for this new market are just those in which England excels, and in which we are, or ought to be, able to defy competition.

Consul Holmwood to James Hutton, 10 April 1885, Public Record Office, F.O. 84/1737.

[b] The country around and beyond Mount Kilimanjaro as far as Lake Victoria Nyanza is the most fertile, healthy and beautiful in Africa. It bounds . . . with produce of great importance to our Commerce. Portions of it have lately been visited by [G. A.] Fischer, a German Traveller and by [Joseph] Thomson and [Harry] Johnston, Englishmen. Fischer is known to be pressing upon the German Government the expediency of possessing themselves of the District.

Some years ago Mr Mackinnon proposed to form an association for developing the wealth of the Continental portions of the Kingdom of Zanzibar. The negotiations came to nothing. [*He suggests that they be revived in the new competitive situation.*] It is believed that there would be no difficulty in obtaining funds for making a Railway to Kilimanjaro; and subsequently to Lake Victoria Nyanza, if such a Concession could be obtained from the Sultan of Zanzibar.

Lord Aberdare to Lord Granville, 24 April 1885, Public Record Office, F.O. 84/1737.

A new Australia as well as a new India

[c] Here is a new country as large as Switzerland, enjoying a singularly fertile soil and healthy climate, capable of producing every vegetable production of the tropical and temperate zonès, free from the tzetze fly, and inhabited sparsely by peaceful agriculturalists, skilled in native manufactures and capable and desirous of instruction: here is a land eminently suited for European colonization, situated near midway between the Equatorial lakes and the Coast. Within a few years it must be either English, French or German. . . . I have only to invite a certain number of chosen

colonists, already desirous of joining my expedition, to come and occupy the beautiful sites which will be given to them gratis, and there to cultivate the vine, the coffee plant, the sugar-cane, rice, wheat, oranges and limes — and the principal points of this healthy district will soon be in the hands of Englishmen. . . . Think what a commanding position this hilly district, with its European climate, occupies in Eastern Equatorial Africa. . . . Situated only 180 miles from the Coast, with an intervening district offering no difficulties whatever in the construction of roads and railways, Kilimanjaro offers an admirable centre for that occupation and colonization of Eastern Africa which must inevitably come from one of the European powers.

Harry Johnston to Lord Edmond Fitzmaurice, Under Secretary for Foreign Affairs, Chàgga, 10 July 1884, quoted Oliver (87), pp. 66-8.

The Government weighs up the possibilities.

[d] The geographical position of the East Coast lays it more within the general area of our foreign policy than that of the West Coast. Our alternative route by the Cape to India may at any time make it important that we should have possession of, or at least free access to, good harbours: the importance is not less since the French movement in Madagascar. The Mahommedan element on the East Coast and the large Indian trade which is there carried on, with its connection, which if not close is none the less real, with all that concerns the Mahommedan world in the Soudan, on the shores of the Red Sea, and on the Hadramaut littoral and Persian Gulf, make it essential that we should secure a preponderating influence over its political future.

Commercially it has made great strides in the 10 years which have elapsed since the Slave export was checked and an impulse given to legitimate trade. Apart from the mineral wealth which is believed to exist between the coast and the great lakes, there is an unlimited capacity for the production of cattle, cereals, and all the usual articles of tropical trade. The climate, even as at present understood, is less unhealthy than that of the West Coast, and the great mountain ranges of Kilimanjaro and Kenia, situated between the lakes which give birth to the Nile & the fine harbours of Zanzibar, afford a European climate and sanatorium within easy reach, if once roads are made, of the coast. It is needless to dwell on the advantages of this to our navy, to our officials, and to traders. There is very good reason, too, for supposing that the natives are more naturally industrious than most of the West Coast tribes, and that they would welcome the establishment of any Government strong enough to enforce good order and prevent the raids of the more turbulent tribes.

Memorandum by Clement Hill, a Foreign Office official, 20 October 1884 (written to assess the implications of the Berlin West Africa Conference for East Africa), Public Record Office, F.O. 84/1813.

document 18
The 'Little Englanders'' stand on Uganda

I am very much exercised in my mind at the news from East Africa and Mombasa. As you will have observed the East African Company have 'thrown up the sponge' (being as I imagine insolvent), and a determined effort is being made to force the British Government to take to the *damnosa haereditas*. Rosebery has circulated a Memo. (for our consideration but not expressing his own sentiments), by Sir P. Anderson (of the F.O.), in the highest jingo tune advocating the annexation of the whole country up to the Albert Lakes with a view to the 'reconquest' of the Sudan via the Upper Nile. . . . Captain Lugard threatens all sorts of horrors if we do not occupy at once. Bishop Tucker swears he will remain at his post and die -- in short every sort of bogey is invoked to involve us in this horrible quagmire, which will be as bad as Khartoum. . . . The railway is *projected* but not *built*, and I hope it never will be. If we embark on this desperate business we shall have no end of trouble with the French and Germans, as indeed we already have. *Cui bono*? Is it *trade*? There is no traffic. Is it *religion*? The Catholics and Protestants (as they call themselves) are occupied in nothing but cutting each other's throats, with their bishops at their head. *Is it slavery*? There is no evidence that there is any slave trade question in this region. . . . I see nothing but endless expense, trouble and disaster in prospect if we allow ourselves to *drift*

133

into any sort of responsibility for this business, and devoutly hope we shall have nothing to do with it.

Sir William Harcourt, Chancellor of the Exchequer, to W. E. Gladstone, 20 September 1892, quoted Gardiner (38), ii, 191-3.

SOUTH AFRICA

document 19

Cecil Rhodes

[a] *The 'First of the Money Kings'*

When Mr Rhodes died, the most conspicuous figure left in the English-speaking race since the death of Queen Victoria disappeared. Whether loved or feared, he towered aloft above all his contemporaries. There are many who hold that he would be entitled to a black statue in the Hall of Eblis. But even those who distrusted and disliked him most, pay reluctant homage to the portentous energy of a character which has affected the world so deeply for weal or woe. . . . It was his distinction to be the first of the new Dynasty of Money Kings which has been evolved in these later days as the real rulers of the modern world. There have been many greater millionaires than he. . . . As a rich man Mr Rhodes was not in the running with Mr Carnegie, Mr Rockefeller, or Mr Astor. But although there have been many wealthier men, none of them, before Mr Rhodes, recognised the opportunities of ruling the world which wealth affords its possessor. The great financiers of Europe have no doubt often used their powers to control questions of peace or war and to influence politics, but they always acted from a strictly financial motive. Their aims were primarily the shifting of the value of stocks. To effect that end they have often taken a leading hand in political deals. But Mr Rhodes inverted the operation. With him political considerations were always paramount. If he used the market he did it in order to secure the means of achieving political ends.

Stead (95), Review of Reviews Office 1902, pp. 51, 55. (*W. T. Stead, a journalist, had been a close associate of Rhodes and Rhodes had intended him to be an executor of his Will until they disagreed about the Boer War.)*

[b] *Rhodes's dream*

I contend that we are the first race in the world, and that the more of the world we inhabit the better it is for the human race. I contend that every acre added to our territory means the birth of more of the English race who otherwise would not be brought into existence. Added to this, the absorption of the greater portion of the world under our rule simply means the end of all wars. . . . The furtherance of the British Empire, for the bringing of the whole uncivilised world under British rule, for the recovery of the United States, for the making the Anglo-Saxon race but one Empire. What a dream! but yet it is probable. It is possible.

Rhodes to W. T. Stead, 19 August 1891, quoted **(95)**, pp. 58-9.

document 20

The Rudd Concession

Know all men by these presents that whereas Charles Dunnell Rudd of Kimberley, Rochfort Maguire of London, and Francis Robert Thompson of Kimberley, herein-after called the grantees, have covenanted and agreed . . . to pay to me my heirs and successors the sum of one hundred pounds sterling British currency on the first day of every lunar month, and further to deliver at my Royal Kraal one thousand Martini-Henry breech-loading rifles, together with one hundred thousand rounds of suitable ball cartridges, five hundred of the said rifles and fifty thousand of the said cartridges to be ordered from England forthwith and delivered with reasonable despatch, and the remainder of the said rifles and cartridges to be delivered so soon as the said grantees shall have commenced to work mining machinery within my territory, and further to deliver on the Zambesi River a steamboat with guns suitable for defensive purposes upon the said river, . . . I, Lo Bengula, King of the Matebele, Mashonaland, and other adjoining territories, in the exercise of my sovereign powers, and in the presence and with the consent of my Council of Indunas, do hereby grant and assign unto the said grantees, their heirs, representatives, and assigns, jointly and severally, the complete and exclusive charge over all metals and minerals situated and contained in my kingdom, . . . together with full powers to do all things that they may deem necessary to win and procure the same, and to hold, collect, and enjoy the profits and revenues . . . and whereas I have been much molested of late by divers persons seeking and desiring to obtain grants and concessions of land and mining rights in my territories, I do hereby authorise the said grantees, . . . to take all necessary and lawful steps to exclude from my kingdoms, . . . all persons seeking land, metals, minerals nor mining rights therein, and I do hereby undertake to render them such needful assistance as they may from time to time require for the exclusion of such persons and to grant no concessions of land or mining rights from and after this date without their consent and concurrence. . . .

This given under my hand this thirtieth day of October in the year of our Lord eighteen hundred and eighty eight at my Royal Kraal.

his

Lo Bengula   X

mark

Parliamentary Papers, li (1890), 545.

document 21

The Colonial Office's doubts about the legality of the British South Africa Company's position

'Matabeleland' is the territory of Lo Bengula, King of the Amandebele or Matabele . . . it had been argued by Bishop Knight Bruce of Bloemfontein and others that Lo Bengula was no more than a marauder, and had no legitimate claims [*over Mashonaland etc.*], but it is too late to go into that now. . . .

It should be premised, as accounting for the recent struggle for the possession of Mashonaland, that the whole country between the Limpopo and the Zambesi had long been reported to be rich in gold . . . after the development of the marvellous gold-fields of Witwatersrand in the Transvaal about 1886-7 . . . it was thought that deposits of ore would be found to recur, equalling or exceeding in riches the deposits of 'the Randt', and the country became the theatre of a lively struggle between speculative groups almost too numerous to mention. . . .

On the 18th of March 1889, the High Commissioner [*Sir Hercules Robinson*] wrote . . . 'The alternatives before us as regards Matabeleland are to recognise a monopoly which may possibly develop into a Royal Charter, or to follow the Swaziland course of allowing a number of competing concession seekers of different nationalities to establish themselves in the country. Lo Bengula would be unable to govern or control such incomers except by a massacre. . . .'

[*On 30 October 1888 Rhodes and his associates obtained the Rudd Concession (doc. 20) and on 29 October 1889 a Royal Charter.*]

It is understood that the concession from Lo Bengula never actually passed, in full proprietary right, to the Chartered Company, but is *leased* by the 'United Concessions Company' [*another company controlled by Rhodes*] to the Chartered Company for a payment of one half the net profits of all their present and prospective undertakings, which, however, have to be conducted entirely at the expense of the Chartered Company. . . .

Sir R. Herbert [*Permanent Under Secretary at the Colonial Office*] wrote, 'It may be safely stated that no persons connected with Her Majesty's Government had any idea that such a scheme was in contemplation when the charter was being considered and settled. If it had been disclosed the charter would certainly have been refused. It may even be a question whether the announcement of it now does not render it necessary to consider whether the charter should be revoked. That would be a very objectionable course, because it would involve the establishment of an administrative protectorate over all the Company's territories. . . . Lord Knutsford [*Colonial Secretary*] wrote . . . 'Although I think we have been misled by the British South Africa Company's founders I am not prepared to take any steps towards putting an end to the charter. This would impose upon this country the responsibility of taking over and administering this enormous territory subject to the concession.'

Memorandum on the Origin and Operations of the British South Africa Chartered Company, 13 October 1892. Public Record Office, C.O. 879/37.

FASHODA AND THE ANGLO-FRENCH AGREEMENTS OF 1904

document 22

The Fashoda incident

[a] *The British case.*

It is desirable that you should be placed in possession of the view of Her Majesty's Government in respect to the line of action to be followed in the event of Khartoum being occupied at an early date by the forces now operating in the Sudan under the command of Sir Herbert Kitchener.

In view of the substantial military and financial co-operation which has recently been afforded by Her Majesty's Government to the Government of the Khedive, Her Majesty's Government have decided that at Khartoum the British and Egyptian flags should be hoisted side by side. This decision will have no reference to the manner in which the occupied countries are to be administered in the future. It is not necessary at present to define their political status with any great precision. . . . You will, however, explain to the Khedive, and to his Ministers that the procedure I have indicated is intended to emphasise the fact that Her Majesty's Government consider that they have a predominant voice in all matters connected with the Soudan, and that they expect that any advice which they may think fit to tender to the Egyptian Government, in respect to Soudan affairs, will be followed. . . .

It is possible that a French force may be found in occupation of some portion of the Nile Valley. Should this contingency arise . . . Her Majesty's Government entertain full confidence in Sir Herbert Kitchener's judgement and discretion. They feel assured that he will endeavour to convince the Commander of any French force with which he may come in contact that the presence of the latter in the Nile Valley is an infringement of the rights of both Great Britain and of the Khedive.

Lord Salisbury to Lord Cromer, 2 August 1898, Secret, Gooch and Temperley, *British Documents on the Origins of the War*, 1898-1914, i, 159-60.

[b] *The French case.*

Fashoda. Minister for Foreign Affairs [*Delcassé*] initiated today a conversation on this burning question by stating that French Minister in London was instructed to speak to your Lordship about it. Much of what passed between us was but a repetition of previous conversations, but his Excellency was just as determined as ever upon the right of France to occupy territory practically abandoned by Egypt and contested the right of Great Britain to warn off other Powers which had not recognised her sphere of influence or to assert that France was committing an unfriendly act in advancing on Upper Nile. He at the same time declared his conviction that honest discussion between the two Governments would soon result in an understanding. He reiterated that it is the desire of the present French Government to make a friend of England, adding that between ourselves he would much prefer an Anglo-French to a Franco-Russian alliance. He again entreated me to take account of existing excitement in France, which is becoming dangerous and might in an instant break out into overt acts, repeating what he had said yesterday: 'Do not ask me for the impossible; do not drive me into a corner.' He admitted that he knew feeling in England is strong, but he argued that Englishmen are not so excitable as the French, and felt sentimental considerations less deeply. I replied that he could not exaggerate strength of feeling in England on this subject, both on the part of the Government and the public, and the knowledge of this caused me great apprehension. He said: 'You surely would not break with us over Fashoda?' To which I answered that it was exactly that which I feared.

Sir E. Monson (British Ambassador in Paris) to Lord Salisbury, 28 September 1898, Telegram, *ibid.*, p. 171.

The Anglo-French Agreements of April 1904

An agreement about colonial questions serves as the basis for a new Anglo-French entente *in European diplomacy.*

His Britannic Majesty's Government declare that they have no intention of altering the political status of Egypt.

The Government of the French Republic, for their part, declare that they will not obstruct the action of Great Britain in that country by asking that a limit of time be fixed for the British occupation or in any other manner, and that they give their assent to the draft Khedivial Decree annexed to the present Arrangement [*for the conversion of the Egyptian debt*].

The Government of the French Republic declare that they have no intention of altering the political status of Morocco.

His Britannic Majesty's Government, for their part, recognise that it appertains to France, more particularly as a Power whose dominions are conterminous for a great distance with those of Morocco, to preserve order in that country, and to provide assistance for the purpose of all administrative, economic, financial, and military reforms which it may require.

They declare that they will not obstruct the action taken by France for this purpose, provided that such action shall leave intact the rights which Great Britain in virtue of Treaties, Conventions, and usage, enjoys in Morocco, including the right of coasting trade between the ports of Morocco, enjoyed by British vessels since 1901.

Articles I and II of the Declaration between the United Kingdom and France respecting Egypt and Morocco, signed at London, 8 April 1904, Gooch and Temperley, *ibid.*, ii, 385-7.

INTERPRETATIONS OF IMPERIALISM

J. A. Hobson

document 24

Hobson argued that the acquisition of a vast new colonial empire in the late nineteenth century had brought little profit to the nation as a whole.

Seeing that the Imperialism of the last six decades is clearly condemned as a bad business policy, in that at enormous expense it had procured a small, bad, unsafe increase of markets, and had jeopardised the entire wealth of the nation in rousing the strong resentment of other nations, we may ask, 'How is the British nation induced to embark upon such unsound business?' The only possible answer is that the business interests of the nation as a whole are subordinated to those of certain sectional interests that usurp control of the national resources and use them for their private gain. . . . Careful analysis of the existing relations between business and politics shows that the aggressive Imperialism which we seek to understand is not in the main the product of blind passions of races or of the mixed folly and ambition of politicians. . . . It is not too much to say that the modern foreign policy of Great Britain has been primarily a struggle for profitable markets of investment. To a larger extent every year Great Britain has been becoming a nation living upon tribute from abroad, and the classes who enjoy this tribute have had an ever-increasing incentive to employ the public policy, the public purse, and the public force to extend the field of their private investment, and to safeguard and improve their existing investments. [None of this would be necessary if mal-distribution of wealth did not lead to chronic under-consumption at home.] It is this economic condition of affairs that forms the taproot of Imperialism. If the consuming public in this country raised its standard of consumption to keep pace with every rise of productive powers, there could be no excess of goods or capital clamorous to use Imperialism in order to find markets. . . . It is not industrial progress that demands the opening up of new markets and areas of investment, but mal-distribution of consuming power which prevents the absorption of commodities and capital within the country.

Hobson (117), pp. 46, 47-50, 53-4, 81, 85.

V. I. Lenin

Capitalism is bound to lead to imperialism and so to its own destruction.

It is characteristic of capitalism in general that the ownership of capital is separated from the application of capital to production, that money capital is separated from industrial or productive capital, and that the rentier who lives entirely on income obtained from money capital, is separated from the entrepreneur and from all who are directly concerned in the management of capital. Imperialism, or the domination of finance capital, is that highest stage of capitalism at which this separation reaches vast proportions. . . .

Typical of the old capitalism, when free competition had undivided sway, was the export of *goods*. Typical of the latest stage of capitalism, when monopolies rule, is the export of *capital*. . . .

It goes without saying that if capitalism . . . could raise the standard of living of the masses, who are everywhere still half-starved and poverty-stricken, in spite of the amazing technical progress, there could be no talk of a surplus, of capital. . . . But if capitalism did these things it would not be capitalism. . . . As long as capitalism remains what it is, surplus capital will be utilized not for the purpose of raising the standard of living of the masses in a given country, for this would mean a decline in profits for the capitalists, but for the purpose of increasing profits by exporting capital abroad to backward countries. . . .

But when nine-tenths of Africa had been seized (by 1900), when the whole world had been divided up, there was inevitably ushered in the era of monopoly ownership of colonies and, consequently, of particularly intense struggle for the division and redivision of the world. . . .

From all that has been said in this book on the economic essence of imperialism, it follows that we must define it as capitalism in transition or, more precisely as moribund capitalism.

Lenin (119), pp. 97-8, 102-4, 214, 218.

document 26
Lord Cromer

The British belief that their rule benefited the world.

No one can fully realise the extent of the change which has come over Egypt since the British occupation took place unless he is in some degree familiar with the system under which the country was governed in the days of Ismail Pasha. The contrast between now and then is, indeed, remarkable. A new spirit has been instilled into the population of Egypt. Even the peasant has learnt to scan his rights. Even the Pasha has learnt that others besides himself have rights which must be respected. The courbash [*whip*] may hang on the walls of the Moudirieh, but the Moudir [*Provincial Governor*] no longer dares to employ it on the backs of the fellaheen. For all practical purposes, it may be said that the hateful corvée system has disappeared. Slavery has virtually ceased to exist. The halcyon days of the adventurer and the usurer are past. Fiscal burthens have been greatly relieved. Everywhere law reigns supreme. Justice is no longer bought and sold. Nature, instead of being spurned and neglected, has been wooed to bestow her gifts on mankind. She has responded to the appeal. The waters of the Nile are now utilised in an intelligent manner. Means of locomotion have been improved and extended. The soldier has acquired some pride in the uniform which he wears. He has fought as he has never fought before. The sick man can be nursed in a well-managed hospital. The lunatic is no longer treated like a wild beast. The punishment awarded to the worst criminal is no longer barbarous. Lastly, the schoolmaster is abroad, with results which are as yet uncertain, but which cannot fail to be important.

Cromer, *Modern Egypt*, ii, 556-7.

A modern rejection of traditional explanations of the Partition

In all the long annals of imperialism, the partition of Africa is a remarkable freak. Few events that have thrown an entire continent into revolution have been brought about so casually.... It used to be supposed that European society must have put out stronger urges to empire in Africa at this time; and all sorts of causes have been suggested to support the supposition. One and all, however, they suffer from a tiresome defect: of powerful new incentives there is remarkably little sign. Only after the partition was long over and done with did capital seek outlets, did industry seek markets in tropical Africa. As late as the end of the century the European economy went on by-passing these poor prospects in favour of the proven fields of America and Asia. Neither is it realistic to explain the movement by some change in the temper of the European mind. The pride and pomps of African empire did not suit the popular taste until late in the 1890s when the partition was all but completed.... Scanning Europe for the causes, the theorists of imperialism have been looking for answers in the wrong places. The crucial changes that set all working took place in Africa itself. It was the fall of an old power [*the Khedivate in Egypt*] in its north, the rise of a new [*the Transvaal*] in its south, that dragged Africa into modern history ... Imbroglios with Egyptian proto-nationalists and thence with Islamic revivals across the whole of the Sudan drew the powers into an expansion of their own in East and West Africa.... The last quarter of the century has often been called the 'Age of Imperialism'. Yet much of this imperialism was no more than an involuntary reaction of Europe to the various proto-nationalisms of Islam that were already rising in Africa against the encroaching thraldom of the white men....

[The gaudy empires spatch-cocked together] have fallen to pieces only three-quarters of a century after being thrown together. It would be a gullible historiography which could see such gimcrack creations as necessary functions of the balance of power or as the highest stage of capitalism.

R. E. Robinson and J. Gallagher, 'The partition of Africa' in *New Cambridge Modern History*, xi, 593-4, 639.

Bibliography

Books

THE AFRICAN BACKGROUND: THE VICTORIAN IMAGE OF
AFRICA

1 Cairns, H. A. C. *Prelude to Imperialism: British reactions to Central African society, 1840-1890*, Routledge, 1965: a very good pioneering study.

2 Curtin, P. D. *The Image of Africa: British ideas and actions, 1780-1850*, Macmillan 1965: a profound study of a complex subject.

3 Davidson, Basil. *Old Africa Rediscovered* (1st edn, 1959), 2nd edn, Longman, 1970: like all Davidson's works an enthusiastic and highly readable reassessment of African history as it is now coming to be understood.

4 Davidson, Basil. *Black Mother: Africa; the years of trial*, Gollancz, 1961: a study of the effects of the Atlantic slave trade.

5 Davidson, Basil. *Africa in History: themes and outlines*, 1st edn (finely illustrated), Weidenfeld & Nicolson, 1966; 2nd edn (text extended but no illustrations), 1968.

6 Davidson, Basil. *The Africans: an entry to cultural history*, Longman, 1969.

7 Gann, L. H. and Duignan, P. *Burden of Empire: an appraisal of Western colonialism in Africa south of the Sahara*, Pall Mall Press, 1968: an unfashionable, but sometimes thought-provoking, rejection of the modern approach to African history.

8 Oliver, R., ed. *The Dawn of African History*, 1st edn, Oxford University Press, 1961: a collection of broadcast talks by Sir Mortimer Wheeler and others; their popularity is demonstrated by the frequency with which they have been reprinted since 1961.

9 Oliver, R., ed. *The Middle Age of African History*, Oxford University Press, 1967: the sequel to (8).

10 Oliver, R. and Fage, J. D. *A Short History of Africa*, 1962, 2nd edn, Penguin, 1966: by far the best short introduction to the subject.

11 Oliver, R. and Atmore, A. *Africa Since 1800*, Oxford University Press, 1967: covers the recent history of Africa in more detail than (10).

12 Oliver, R. and Oliver, C., eds. *Africa in the Days of Exploration*, Prentice-Hall, Spectrum Books, 1965: an anthology.

13 Perham, M. and Simmons, J., eds. *African Discovery: an anthology of exploration* (1st edn, 1942), 2nd edn, Faber, 1963.

14 Pope-Hennessy, James. *Sins of the Fathers: the Atlantic slave traders, 1441-1807*, Weidenfeld & Nicolson, 1967; Sphere Books, 1970.

15 Richardson, Patrick. *Empire and Slavery*, Longman, 1968.

16 Trimingham, John. *The Influence of Islam upon Africa*, Longman, 1968.

17 Underwood, Leon. *Bronzes of West Africa*, Tiranti, 1949.

18 Williams, Eric. *Capitalism and Slavery* (1st edn, 1944), 2nd edn, Deutsch, 1964.

THE SCRAMBLE FOR AFRICA

19 Aldcroft, D. H., ed. *The Development of British Industry and Foreign Competition, 1875-1914*, Allen & Unwin, 1968: a useful collection of essays.

20 Andrew, C. *Théophile Delcassé and the Making of the Entente Cordiale*, Macmillan, 1968.

21 Anstey, Roger. *Britain and the Congo in the Nineteenth Century*, Oxford, Clarendon Press, 1962.

22 Ascherson, N. *The King Incorporated*, Allen & Unwin, 1963: a highly critical study of Leopold II.

23 Aydelotte, W. O. *Bismarck and British Colonial Policy*, Oxford University Press, 1937.

24 Blake, Robert. *Disraeli*, Eyre & Spottiswoode, 1966.

25 Blunt, Wilfrid Scawen. *Secret History of the English Occupation of Egypt*, Unwin, 1907: a partisan account but with much genuine 'inside information'.

26 Cecil, Lady Gwendolen. *Life of Robert, Marquis of Salisbury*, 4 vols, Hodder & Stoughton, 1921-32.

27 Churchill, Winston S. *The River War: the reconquest of the Sudan*, (1899); Four Square Books, 1960.

28 Colvin, Auckland. *The Making of Modern Egypt*, Seeley, 1906: the account of a high-ranking British official.

29 Coupland, R. *The Exploitation of East Africa, 1856-1890: the slave trade and the Scramble* (1st edn, 1939), Faber, 1968: still important, based on the papers of Sir John Kirk.

30 Cromer, Lord. *Modern Egypt*, 2 vols, Macmillan, 1908: the classic British account by the man who was virtually governor of Egypt, 1883-1907.

31 Crowe, S. E. *The Berlin West Africa Conference, 1884-1885*, Longmans, 1942: still by far the best study of the Conference.

32 Dike, K. O. *Trade and Politics in the Niger Delta, 1830-1885*, Oxford, Clarendon Press, 1956: a pioneering study by an eminent African historian.

33 Fage, J. D. *An Introduction to the History of West Africa*, Cambridge University Press, 1955; paperback, 1962: short and useful.

34 Farnie, D. A. *East and West of Suez: the Suez Canal in history, 1854-1956*, Oxford, Clarendon Press, 1969: a massive study.

35 Fitzmaurice, Lord Edmond. *The Life of Lord Granville, 1815-1891*, 2 vols, Longmans, 1906.

36 Flint, J. E. *Sir George Goldie and the Making of Nigeria,* Oxford University Press, 1960.

37 Fyfe, C. *A History of Sierra Leone*, Oxford, Clarendon Press, 1962.

38 Gardiner, A. G. *The Life of Sir William Harcourt,* 2 vols, Constable, 1923.

39 Garvin, J. L. and Amery, J. *Life of Joseph Chamberlain*, 6 vols, Macmillan, 1935-69.

40 Gifford, P. and Louis, W. R., eds. *Britain and Germany in Africa: imperial rivalry and colonial rule*, Yale University Press, 1967: a useful collection of essays.

41 Grenville, J. A. S. *Lord Salisbury and Foreign Policy: the close of the nineteenth century*, Athlone Press, 1964.

42 Grey, Lord. *Twenty-Five Years, 1892-1916*, Hodder & Stoughton, 1926.

43 Gwynn, S. and Tuckwell, G. M. *The Life of Sir Charles W. Dilke*, 2 vols, Murray, 1917.

44 Hallett, Robin, ed. *Records of the African Association, 1788-1831*, Nelson, 1964.

45 Halperin, V. *Lord Milner and the Empire: the evolution of British imperialism*, Odhams Press, 1952.

46 Hanna, A. J. *The Story of the Rhodesias and Nyasaland*, Faber, 1960.

47 Hargreaves, John. *Prelude to the Partition of West Africa*, Macmillan, 1963: an important study.

48 Henderson, W. O. *Studies in German Colonial History*, Cass, 1962.

49 Herold, J. C. *Bonaparte in Egypt*, Hamish Hamilton, 1962.

50 Holt, P. *The Mahdist State in the Sudan, 1881-1898*, Oxford, Clarendon Press, 1958.

51 Hoskins, H. L. *British Routes to India* (1928); reprint, Cass, 1966.

52 Imlah, A. H. *Economic Elements in the Pax Britannica: studies in British foreign trade in the nineteenth century*, Harvard University Press, 1958.

53 Ingham, K. *A History of East Africa*, 2nd edn, Longmans, 1963: the best short history.

54 Ingham, K. *The Making of Modern Uganda*, Allen & Unwin, 1958.

55 Jackson, S. *The Great Barnato*, Heinemann, 1970: an exceptionally lively biography.

56 James, Robert Rhodes. *Rosebery*, Weidenfeld & Nicolson, 1964.

57 Jones, G. I. *The Trading States of the Oil Rivers*, Oxford University Press, 1963: important because it studies the African politics of the region.

58 Kanya-Forstner, A. S. *The Conquest of the Western Sudan: a study in French military imperialism*, Cambridge University Press, 1969: the first good study in English of this subject which covers a much wider field than French military history.

59 Keppel-Jones, Arthur. *South Africa: a short history*, Hutchinson, 1949; 4th edn, Hutchinson, 1963: the best short introduction.

60 Kiewiet, C. W. De, *The Imperial Factor in South Africa*, Cambridge University Press, 1937.

61 Kimble, D. *A Political History of Ghana: the rise of Gold Coast nationalism 1850-1928*, Oxford, Clarendon Press, 1963: an important modern study.

62 Langer, W. L. *European Alliance and Alignments, 1871-1890; The Diplomacy of Imperialism, 1890-1902* (1931, 1935), 2nd edn, Knopf, 1950.

63 Le May, G. H. L. *British Supremacy in South Africa, 1899-1907*, Oxford, Clarendon Press, 1963.

64 Lockhart, J. G. and Woodhouse, C. M. *Rhodes*, Hodder & Stoughton, 1963: the latest major biography of Rhodes.

65 Lowe, C. J. *The Reluctant Imperialists: British foreign policy, 1878-1902*, Routledge, 1967: a comprehensive study that includes much that is relevant to Africa.

66 McCoan, J. C. *Egypt As It Is*, Cassell, 1877: an exceptionally well-informed contemporary account by an Irish journalist.

67 McIntyre, W. D. *The Imperial Factor in the Tropics, 1865-75*,

Macmillan, 1967: much of this book is concerned with Asia but there are interesting sections on West Africa.

68 Mackenzie Wallace, D. *Egypt and the Egyptian Question*, Macmillan, 1883: a contemporary analysis by a well-known journalist.

69 Magnus, Philip. *Gladstone*, Murray, 1954 (paperback 1963): a convenient one-volume 'Life'.

70 Magnus, Philip. *Kitchener: portrait of an imperialist*, Murray, 1958; Penguin, 1968.

71 Mansfield, Peter. *The British in Egypt*, Weidenfeld & Nicolson, 1971: covers the period from 1882 to 1956.

72 Marlowe, John. *Anglo-Egyptian Relations, 1800-1953*, Cresset, 1954.

73 Marlowe, John. *The Making of the Suez Canal*, Cresset, 1964.

74 Marlowe, John. *Cromer in Egypt*, Elek, 1970.

75 Mason, Philip: *The Birth of a Dilemma: the conquest and settlement of Rhodesia*, Oxford University Press, 1958: an outstanding study of this difficult question.

76 Medlicott, W. N. *Bismarck, Gladstone and the Concert of Europe.* Athlone Press, 1956.

77 Milner, Alfred. *England in Egypt,* Arnold, 1892: an exposition of the benefits British rule had conferred on Egypt.

78 Monger, G. W. *The End of Isolation: British foreign policy, 1900-1907*, Nelson, 1963.

79 Morel, E. D. *Red Rubber*, Unwin, 1906; reprint New York, Haskell, 1970.

80 Morley, John. *Life of Gladstone*, 3 vols, Macmillan, 1903.

81 Morris, Donald R. *The Washing of the Spears*, Cape, 1966; Sphere Books, 1968.

82 Newbury, C. W. *The Western Slave Coast and its Rulers*, Oxford, Clarendon Press, 1961.

83 Ninet, J. *Arabi Pacha*, Paris, 1884: an account by a friend and close associate of the Egyptian leader.

84 Nutting, A. *Gordon: martyr and misfit,* Constable, 1966: a stimulating biography.

85 Nutting, A. *Scramble for Africa: the Great Trek to the Boer War*, Constable, 1970: a rather misleading title since the book is entirely concerned with Southern Africa.

86 Oliver, R. and Mathew, G., eds. *History of East Africa*, vol. i, Harlow, V. and Chilver, E. M., eds. *History of East Africa,* vol. ii, Oxford, Clarendon Press, 1963, 1965: a collection of essays by well-known authorities.

87 Oliver, R. *Sir Harry Johnston and the Scramble for Africa*, Chatto & Windus, 1957.

88 Oxford History of South Africa, ed. M. Wilson and L. Thompson, vol. i, *South Africa to 1870*, Oxford, Clarendon Press, 1969.

89 Pakenham, E. *Jameson's Raid*, Weidenfeld & Nicolson, 1960.

90 Perham, Margery *Lugard: the Life of Frederick Dealtry Lugard*, vol. i, *The Years of Adventure, 1858-1898*; vol. ii, *The Years of Authority, 1898-1945*, Collins, 1956, 1960.

91 Peters, Karl. *King Solomon's Golden Ophir*, trans. F. Karuth, Leadenhall Press, 1899.

92 van der Poel, J. *The Jameson Raid*, Oxford, Clarendon Press, 1951.

93 Pudney, John. *Suez: De Lesseps Canal*, Dent, 1968.

94 Redford, A. *Manchester Merchants and Foreign Trade*, vol. ii, 1850-1939, Manchester University Press, 1956.

95 Rhodes, Cecil. *The Last Will and Testament of Cecil J. Rhodes*, ed. W. T. Stead, *Review of Reviews* Office, 1902.

96 Robinson, R. and Gallagher, J. *Africa and the Victorians: the official mind of imperialism*, Macmillan, 1961: a very important new interpretation.

97 Robson, R. *The Cotton Industry in Britain*, Macmillan, 1957.

98 Rothstein, T. *Egypt's Ruin*, A. C. Fifield, 1910: an important near-contemporary criticism of British actions.

99 Rudin, H. R. *The Germans in the Cameroons, 1884-1918*, Cape, 1938.

100 Sabri, Mustapha. *La Genèse de l'Ésprit National Égyptien 1863-1882*, Paris, 1924.

101 Sanderson, G. N. *England, Europe and the Upper Nile, 1882-1899*, Edinburgh University Press, 1965.

102 Saul, S. B. *The Myth of the Great Depression* (Studies in Economic History), Macmillan, 1969: a very useful short discussion with bibliography.

103 Saul, S. B. *Studies in British Overseas Trade, 1870-1914*, Liverpool University Press, 1960.

104 Taylor, A. J. P. *Germany's First Bid for Colonies, 1884-1885*, Macmillan, 1938.

105 Taylor, A. J. P. *The Struggle for the Mastery in Europe*, Oxford, Clarendon Press, 1954.

106 Temperley, H. W. V. *England and the Near East: the Crimea* (1936), reprinted, Cass, 1964.

107 Townsend, M. E. *The Rise and Fall of Germany's Colonial Empire* (1930), 2nd edn, Howard Fertig, 1966.

108 Walker, E. A. *A History of Southern Africa* (1928), 3rd rev. edn, Longmans, 1962.
109 Ward, W. E. F. *A History of the Gold Coast*, 2nd edn, Allen & Unwin, 1958.
110 Williams, Basil. *Cecil Rhodes,* Constable, 1921: still the classic biography of Rhodes which, in many ways, has never been surpassed.

CONCLUSIONS

111 Bodelsen, C. A. *Studies in Mid-Victorian Imperialism* (1924), reprint, Heinemann, 1960.
112 Brailsford, H. N. *The War of Steel and Gold*, Bell, 1914.
113 Brown, B. H. *The Tariff Reform Movement in Great Britain, 1881-1895*, Columbia University Press, 1943.
114 Brunschwig, H. *French Colonialism 1871-1914: myths and realities*, trans. W. G. Brown, Pall Mall Press, 1966: a stimulating discussion.
115 Fieldhouse, D. K. *The Theory of Capitalist Imperialism*, Longmans, 1967: a collection of documents with useful introduction.
116 Hancock, W. K. *Wealth of Colonies*, Cambridge University Press: an important critique of Marxist theories.
117 Hobson, J. A. *Imperialism: a study* (1902), 3rd rev. edn, Allen & Unwin, 1938: a book of first class importance and very readable.
118 Koebner, R. and Schmidt, D. H. *Imperialism: a political word, 1840-1960*, Cambridge University Press, 1964: a very important and enlightening study.
119 Lenin, V. I. *Imperialism, the Highest Stage of Capitalism* (1917); reprints inc. Moscow, Foreign Languages Publishing House, n.d.: the classic Marxist statement.
120 Lugard, F. *The Dual Mandate in British Tropical Africa* (1922), reprinted, Cass, 1965.
121 Mellor, G. R. *British Imperial Trusteeship, 1783-1850*, Faber, 1951.
122 Moon, P. T. *Imperialism and World Politics* (1926), Macmillan, 1962: an American view much read between the wars.
123 Morris, James. *Pax Britannica*, Faber, 1968: a readable anthology of the British Empire in 1897.
124 Platt, D. C. M. *Finance, Trade and Politics: British Foreign Policy, 1815-1914*, Oxford University Press, 1968: an important modern study casting doubt *inter alia* on the importance of financiers in policy making.

125 Schumpeter, J. A. *Capitalism, Socialism, and Democracy*, Allen & Unwin, 1942; 3rd edn, 1950: Schumpeter was one of the few writers to attack economic explanations of imperialism in the inter-war period.

126 Semmel, Bernard. *Imperialism and Social Reform*, Allen & Unwin, 1960: an important study of the interaction of the two.

127 Strachey, John. *End of Empire*, Gollancz, 1959: a stimulating discussion.

128 Woolf, Leonard. *Empire and Commerce in Africa* (1920), reprinted, Allen & Unwin, 1968.

Articles

129 Anstey, R. T. 'Capitalism and slavery: a critique', *Economic History Review*, 2nd ser., xxi, 1968.

130 Brunschwig, H. 'Les origines du partage de l'Afrique occidentale', *Journal of African History*, v, 1964.

131 Bury, J. P. T. 'Gambetta and overseas problems', *English Historical Review*, lxxxii, 1967.

132 Drus, E. 'The Question of Imperial Complicity in the Jameson Raid', *English Historical Review*, lxviii, 1953.

133 Fieldhouse, D. K. ' "Imperialism": an historiographical revision', *Economic History Review,* 2nd ser., siv, 1961.

134 Gillard, D. R. 'Salisbury's African policy and the Heligoland offer of 1890', *English Historical Review*, lxxv, 1960.

135 Gillard, D. R. 'Salisbury's Heligoland offer: the case against the Witu thesis', *English Historical Review*, lxxx, 1965.

136 Hardy, S. M. 'Joseph Chamberlain and some problems of the "under-developed estates",' *University of Birmingham Historical Journal*, xi, 1968.

137 Koebner, R. 'The concept of economic imperialism', *Economic History Review, 2nd ser., ii, 1949.*

138 Louis, W. R. 'Sir Percy Anderson's grand African strategy, 1883-96', *English Historical Review*, lxxxi, 1966.

139 Newbury, C. W. 'Victorians, republicans and the partition of Africa', *Journal of African History*, iii, 1962.

140 Newbury, C. W. 'The development of French policy on the Lower and Upper Niger, 1880-1898', *Journal of Modern History*, xxxi, 1959.

141 Newbury, C. W. and Kanya-Forstner, A. S. 'French policy and the origins of the Scramble for West Africa', *Journal of African History*, x, 1969.

142 Newbury, C. W. 'The Protectionist revival in French colonial trade: the case of Senegal', *Economic History Review,* 2nd ser., xxi, 1968.

143 Platt, D. C. M. 'The imperialism of free trade: some reservations', *Economic History Review*, 2nd ser., xxi, 1968.

144 Platt, D. C. M. 'Economic factors in British policy during the "New Imperialism"', *Past and Present*, xxxix, 1968.

145 Robinson, R. and Gallagher, J. 'The imperialism of free trade', *Economic History Review*, 2nd ser., vi, 1953.

146 Robinson, R. and Gallagher, J. 'The Partition of Africa', in *New Cambridge Modern History*, vol. xi, Cambridge University Press, 1962.

147 Sanderson, G. N. 'The Anglo-German agreement of 1890 and the Upper Nile', *English Historical Review*, lxxviii, 1963.

148 Stembridge, S. R. 'Disraeli and the millstones', *Journal of British Studies*, v, 1965.

149 Stengers, J. 'L'Imperialisme colonial de la fin du XIX siècle: mythe ou realité?', *Journal of African History*, iii, 1962: trans. in P. J. M. McEwan, ed. *Readings in African History*, vol. ii, Oxford University Press, 1968.

150 Stokes, E. 'Great Britain and Africa: the myth of imperialism', *History Today*, x, 1960.

151 Stokes, E. 'Late nineteenth-century colonial expansion and the attack on the theory of economic imperialism: a case of mistaken identity?', *Historical Journal*, xii, 1969.

152 von Strandmann, H. Pogge. 'The domestic origins of Germany's colonial expansion under Bismarck', *Past and Present*, xlii, 1969.

153 Wehler, H-U. 'Bismarck's Imperialism, 1862-1890', *Past and Present*, xlviii, 1970: a useful summary of his massive *Bismarck und der Imperialismus*, Kiepenheuer & Witsch 1969.

ADDENDA

The following useful books have become available since the present work went to Press:

Cooke, James J. *New French Imperialism 1880-1910: The Third Republic and Colonial Expansion*, David and Charles, 1973.

Gifford, P. and Louis, W. R., eds. *France and Britain in Africa: imperial rivalry and colonial rule*, Yale University Press.

Latham, A. J. H. *Old Calabar 1600-1891: the impact of the international economy upon a traditional society*, Oxford, Clarendon Press, 1973.

Hallett, Robin. *Africa since 1875: a modern history*, Ann Arbor, University of Michigan Press, 1974.

Hargreaves, John. *West Africa Partitioned*, vol. 1, *The Loaded Pause, 1885–1809*, Macmillan, 1974.

The Cambridge History of Africa (eds. R.A. Cliver and J.D. Fage), vols 3–5, Cambridge University Press, 1975–7.

Index

Index